Nature Walks in Southern Vermont

An AMC Nature Walks Book

Mark Mikolas

APPALACHIAN MOUNTAIN CLUB BOOKS
BOSTON, MASSACHUSETTS

Cover Photograph: Kindra Clineff
Book and Map Design: Carol Bast Tyler
All photographs by the author unless otherwise indicated.

Distributed by The Globe Pequot Press, GPP., Inc.,
Old Saybrook, CT.

Library of Congress Cataloging-in-Publication Data

The paper used in this publication meets the minimum requirements of the American National Standard for Information Sciences—Permanence of Paper for Printed Library Materials, ANSI Z39.48–1984.∞

**Due to changes in conditions, use of the information
in this book is at the sole risk of the user.**

Printed on recycled paper using soy-based inks.
Printed in the United States of America.

10 9 8 7 6 5 4 3 2 1   95 96 97 98 99

Also available from AMC Books

Nature Walks in Eastern Massachusetts
Mike Tougias

Nature Walks in Southern New Hampshire
Julia Older and Steve Sherman

Nature Hikes in the White Mountains
Robert Buchsbaum

Quiet Water Canoe Guide: New Hampshire/Vermont
Alex Wilson

Quiet Water Canoe Guide:
Massachusetts/Connecticut/Rhode Island
Alex Wilson

Quiet Water Canoe Guide: Maine
Alex Wilson and John Hayes

Quiet Water Canoe Guide: Pennsylvania
Scott and Linda Shalaway

Nature Walks
in Southern
Vermont

An AMC Nature Walks Book

Contents

Nature Essays

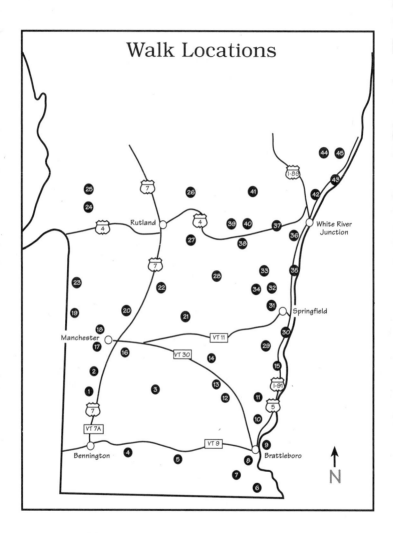

Walk Locations

Rutland

White River
Junction

Springfield

Manchester

VT 11

VT 30

Bennington

VT 7A

VT 9

Brattleboro

N

Key to Walk Locations

Stop. Look. Listen.
—Les Blank, documentary filmmaker

Dedicated to the memory of my Dad.
He awakened my interest in Mother Nature.
He taught me how nurturing she can be.
He was always there to help.
And he walks with me still.

Introduction

Nita Harrison is a wildflower lover and nature photographer. We were walking a trail along the West River together when she noticed jack-in-the-pulpits off to the side. I missed them, but looking out through the trees, spotted an osprey nesting platform.

At North Springfield Lake, I gazed at the river valley below, imagining it when it was fully flooded in 1984. At the same time, Eleanor Ellis—who led the Ascutney Audubon Society's creation of the Springweather Nature Area—identified a distant warbler by ear.

I was searching for chestnut sprouts along a trail when my fellow hiker and fungus-forager, Iva Wood, stopped me from stepping on a destroying angel—the beautifully but deadly poisonous mushroom also known as the angel of death.

Anne Tobey, a fearless and faithful participant in our Sunday AM Amblers walking group, pointed out a trailing arbutus right in front of me as I was contemplating the shape of the rock face of a ledge.

When we came to an almost solid cover of small pines in a clearing, I saw the graceful way the light fell on them. Bill Guenther—friend, forester, and smokeater—looked at the same pines, but he saw them as evidence of an especially bountiful seed crop five years earlier.

My wife Patti and I were walking around our pond. I spotted the tracks of a moose, while she watched a flicker return to its nest in a dead birch tree.

Gary Salmon—forester, trout fisherman, and mean editor to boot—read my write-up of a trail that he often leads groups on. His comment was, "Boy, do we see different trees!"

How much you see depends on what you know

Seeing is a very personal activity. It doesn't just happen. Our attention is powerfully directed to those things we've learned to recognize, understand, and appreciate.

An anthropologist once performed an experiment in seeing. He selected a "boring" photograph of a desert and showed it to many subjects and asked, "What do you see?"

Most people replied by saying, "A desert, some cactuses…that's about it."

Then he showed it to an elderly Navajo man and asked him, "What do you see?"

The Navajo looked at the picture quietly for a while and then began describing what he saw: "The berries are starting to form on the cactus, so it must be early June. From the shadows and the direction of those high, wispy clouds, I'd say we're looking northwest at about four o'clock in the afternoon. It must have rained pretty well earlier in the spring, so my guess is that this picture was taken the year before last.

"That black stain on the rocks is from the droppings of a jumping mouse. His nest must be nearby…let me see...there it is; it's that little mound of branches and debris under the mesquite...." And on he continued.

The more you know, the more you see, but no subject seems more inexhaustible than nature.

The easiest way to learn about nature is to spend time outdoors with people whose knowledge and experience extend beyond our own. Opportunities to spend time with such people are not always possible, but the nature walks in this book were all conceived and created by people with specialized knowledge and the willingness to share their understanding of the natural world through the hard toil of trail building. There is much to be learned by walking and observing them, but if we had a chance to walk them with a specialist, our learning and seeing appreciate even more quickly.

This guide is an effort to provide you with just such an opportunity. Actually it affords you a chance to do much more than walk with an expert—for I would never describe myself that way. Instead, it provides the reader with dozens of expert guides: naturalists, geologists, botanists, birders, foresters, mycophiles, surveyors, entomologists, environmental educators, rangers, historians, and more. People from all of these walks of life—professionals and amateurs alike—graciously and generously shared their knowledge, time, and experience with us. And joining them are all the people who have written and illustrated brochures and books, those who created wonderfully informative maps, performed research and published their learning, and people who prepared in-depth inventories and management plans for many of the areas in which the walks are located.

The people who answered our many questions and cleared up our many confusions, who offered their time to read our drafts and correct and educate us, number far too many to mention individually, and I wouldn't want to single anyone out without singling out everyone. Suffice it to say that every person we contacted in the course of researching this book enthusiastically supported—and substantially contributed to—our effort. My role has been that of a midwife, passing on their knowledge and experience to the reader.

The decisiveness, intelligence, and flexibility of our editor and publisher, Gordon Hardy, made it a joy for us to work with him—even under the most pressing circumstances. We appreciate equally the support and hard work contributed by his staff, Carol Tyler and Carrie Loats, and copyeditor Patricia Welch.

Who is "we"?

The "we" used throughout this guide is not a royal we. It refers to my wife, Patti, and me. Patti likes to stay in the background, but she really did most of the work on this book—I only wrote it. And she and I walked together on every trail but one, where she more wisely stayed back while I forded a freezing stream barefoot.

I've been hiking and camping my whole life; Patti came to her love of the outdoors later in life. I relish roughing it; Patti loves B&Bs. For vacations, I go into the wilderness alone; Patti prefers London. I'll walk five or ten miles and climb a couple of thousand feet just for the sake of being in the woods; to Patti, a walk is a mile or two on a level trail with an interesting destination.

Thus, Patti adds a valuable perspective to my own. I suspect that far more readers will probably share her viewpoint than mine—especially in judging the difficulty and appeal of the trails.

Rating the walks

We use the conventional rating system of *very easy, easy, moderate, difficult,* but how we determined the rating is quite different from most hiking guides. We rated these trails by how Patti would think of them, not how I would. Below is the result:

Very easy: Short and level, with an improved footpath. Thus, even someone who needs assistance to walk, such as using a cane, can still enjoy it. Chances are that if you can get out of bed and stand up, you can take a walk we've rated *very easy.*

Easy: Perhaps a little longer, relatively level, but not necessarily a smooth footpath. Even if you're the type of person who doesn't own a pair hiking boots, you can enjoy an *easy* walk.

Moderate: Longer and involving some up-and-down walking, perhaps as much as 300 to 400 feet of climbing. The footing is generally rougher (rocks, roots, soft spots, etc.). Just about anybody can do a *moderate* walk, but not everybody can enjoy it.

Difficult: Several miles or more in length. There may be as much as 900 to 1000 feet of ascent, and/or involving steep slopes and poor footing. Unless you consider walking uphill fun, a *difficult* walk is probably not for you.

The time given for each walk is based on Patti's pace more than mine. Often a range is given. The lower end represents a stroll through, while the upper end includes time spent stopping to observe features along the way. There is a great deal of latitude in judging how much time you may spend on a particular walk. A fit walker can cover two miles in 30 or 40 minutes. In the North Springfield Bog, on the other hand, you can easily spend that much time just observing its plantlife, while walking only a couple of hundred feet.

What to bring

Going for a nature walk doesn't require the planning and packing that a day hike might, but it is wise to give it some thought. Under the heading of each walk, we have drawn attention to items that are especially important to fully appreciate a particular locale.

However, when it comes to preparing for any venture outdoors, whether a quarter-mile on a trail or 10 miles, the only mistake is leaving something behind that you might need; it's *never* a mistake to have it with you.

I suggest that the easiest way to stay organized for trail walking (if you do it regularly) is to select one small pack and put everything in it you *might* need, even if only rarely. I never unpack this pack—I just grab it, throw in a bottle of water, and head out the door. That way, I never have to worry about whether I'm forgetting something. For example, it may not rain today, but on a day when it does rain unexpectedly, I always have the right gear with me. I'm also prepared to help anyone I meet who might need assistance. Maybe after all my years of being a Boy Scout, *Be prepared* just comes naturally.

Below are the items that always remain in my pack:

- A small pair of binoculars.
- Bug repellent.
- A small flashlight to peer into dens and cavities and for emergencies.
- A magnifying glass or loupe.
- A compass and map for the area I'm walking in.
- A tape measure for measuring such things as animal footprints, tree circumference, wildflower blooms, etc.
- Extra film and batteries.
- Notebook and pen, and business cards (for exchanging addresses with people I might meet).
- A compact windbreaker/rain jacket (which provides extra warmth if needed and can serve as a seat cushion when sitting somewhere damp).
- TP, a small medical kit, a whistle, waterproof matches, and a couple of bandannas are always there as well. I use them rarely, but when I've needed them, they've been indispensable.
- I always carry drinking water. I've had to share it with less-prepared hikers, and I've used it to wash cuts if someone's injured.

The majority of the walks in this book can be done in any comfortable footwear, but when hiking boots or waterproof footwear is mentioned, it's because they are important to enjoying the walk. 'Nuff said.

Read me first!

The Prospect Rock and Wantastiquet Mountain walks both require long climbs. Though they are more ambitious than the remaining trails in this guide, they offer unique bird's-eye perspectives. From these two vantage points, much of southern Vermont can be seen. Whether these are your kinds of walks or not, I suggest at least reading the accounts of each, because from these perspectives, the big picture of the lay of the land is discussed.

Throughout this guide we have tried to convey the interrelationships that underlie an understanding of nature. For instance, just as birds and mammals live in particular habitats, wildflowers and trees and fungi and shrubs and weeds all grow where they grow for a reason. Their existence in a particular place can only be explained by relating it to such factors as climate (on both the macro- and microscale), sunlight and shade, the aspect of the slope, past use of the land, and a multitude of soil factors, such as dampness, depth, pH, compaction, and cyclic changes throughout the year. All of these factors, in turn, are related to the big picture: the lay of the land.

By reading the accounts of these two walks and their accompanying essays, we hope to introduce you to the overall geologic context of southern Vermont's rivers and gorges, its mountains, lakes, rivers, and valleys. For example, every part of Vermont was profoundly shaped and affected by the glacial sheet that covered the state as recently as 12,000 years ago.

The cross-referencing of walks throughout the book is intended to reveal the links among many natural factors, so that the fabric and web of natural existence can be seen in the same seamless way it exists. Remember, if you take a number of the walks recounted in this guide, you will not be seeing *different places*; you are merely seeing *different parts of one big place*.

And then, if you are lucky, on one of your walks one day, you will stop seeing trees and flowers and ferns and earth and lichens and fungi and rocks and vistas and birds and insects and amphibians and mammals and water; and you'll stop worrying about whether you know the popular and scientific names, the reproductive mechanisms, the lifecycles, the nutritional requirements, and the habits of the living things around you...and for just that one moment...

And here I'll take the advice of philosopher Ludwig Wittgenstein: "Things about which we can say nothing, let us therefore remain silent."

Hours, fees, and regulations

Many of our walks are in Vermont state parks, on U.S. Army Corps of Engineer lands at dam sites, or in the Green Mountain National Forest (GMNF). Because operating hours, restrictions, and possible fees are subject to change, we did not list them with each walk, other than when it might affect your planning.

Where necessary, a call ahead is in order. The address and phone number of all organizations mentioned in the guide are provided in Appendix C.

Vermont State Parks

Vermont state parks in the southern and central areas of the state generally open mid-May and close in early October. Dates change from year to year and from park to park. If you are making plans at the very beginning or end of the season, check with the appropriate office of the Vermont Department of Parks and Recreation, listed with each walk under *Affiliated Organizations.*

There are fees to enter all of the state parks, with the exception of Sweet Pond.

Where trails can be walked without entering the park, such as Gifford Woods and Glen Lake Trail, we have indicated where cars can be parked.

With the exception of guide dogs, no dogs are allowed in day-use areas or parking lots of state parks, nor are they permitted at the Montshire Nature Trails.

Although most state park access gates, as well as those at U.S. Army Corps of Engineers dam sites, are locked during the closed season, all can be entered on foot. If an access road is so long that you might not want to walk in, we have mentioned it. When parking at a park whose gate is closed, do not block the gate.

Most state parks offer additional recreational opportunities, such as camping, picnicking, swimming, fishing, and boating.

U.S. Army Corps of Engineers (dams)

In 1995, there was no fee to enter U.S. Army Corps of Engineer lands and recreation areas, with the exception of North Hartland Lake, where fees are only being charged for people who plan to swim or launch a boat.

The mountain laurel in bloom on the granite dome of Black Mountain.

The fee policy for individual dams is set annually by headquarters in Washington, D.C. and is subject to the same indecipherable vagaries associated with any institution headquartered in that fair city. Call the individual dam site to obtain information ahead of time.

No dogs are allowed at dam sites unless physically restrained. Leashes must be six feet or less in length.

Green Mountain National Forest

Access and fee information are given in individual nature walks.

Selecting walks

The quick reference chart of walks and highlights at the back of this book indicates the difficulty of each walk and the particular subject areas for which it is best suited. Thus, if you have a particular interest, you can select walks that will most appeal to you. Mushrooms have not been included, since they are ubiquitous and depend on extremely local conditions. Other interests, such as birds and wildflowers, may be pursued almost anywhere as well, but we have marked those walks that offer the best opportunities for either unique or a wide variety of sightings.

In many cases, a trail is given two ratings of difficulty. In all cases, the easier walk may be taken, while avoiding the more difficult trail or trail section. See each trail write-up for details.

Bennington Area

Healing Springs Nature Trail
Shaftsbury State Park

- **1 mile, several very short but steep sections**
- **45 minutes**
- **easy**
- **bring binoculars**

If you can only do one walk in this book, this is not a bad one to choose. It offers great diversity in a short distance and a rare chance to walk on a glacial esker.

This trail was such a pleasure to walk that my first inclination was simply to write, "Forget all the identifications and explanations. Just walk it and *enjoy* nature rather than studying it." However, knowing there may be a few armchair trail walkers out there, let's start off around the lake.

The trail begins to the right of the dam, where we cut down the bank to follow the shore. It leads across private property, and passes a huge **cottonwood** tree, its branches hanging lazily over the water. Cottonwood, like its other relatives in the poplar family, is a relative-

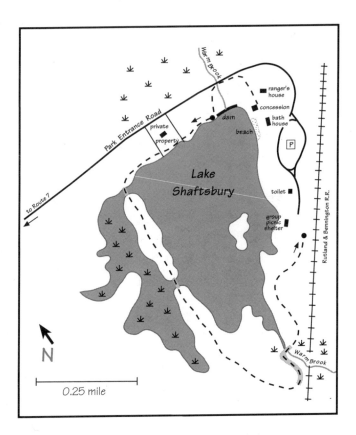

ly short-lived tree. It compensates for its short life however, by being our fastest-growing tree, able to grow 60
feet high in 15 years.

At the end of Lake Shaftsbury, the trail turns left
over a small bridge and leads to one of my all-time

The southern end of Lake Shaftsbury provides an excellent example of the successive transitions from open water to a tree swamp.

favorite stretches of trail. I am an inveterate ridge-walk lover. Generally that means climbing a mountain most of the morning and then hiking along a ridge until it is time to descend. This trail climbs to a mini-ridge-walk, in the form of an **esker** (see page 8). At its beginning is a **beech/hemlock forest.** The pathway curves gracefully back and forth between the boles of large trees, and the land falls away abruptly on either side, creating a top-of-the-world feeling. Your feet tread on a soft organic mat dotted with rounded cobbles, much different from the angular chunks of stone usually found in Vermont. It is a sweet little stretch of trail that I only wish were miles longer.

We descended to a little bridge that connects the island with the finger of land, where there is a transition to an **oak hardwood forest.** On our right, a large marsh offers excellent waterfowl watching. We were there early in the season and saw pairs of **wood ducks** and **mallards.** Male wood ducks—with iridescent head and swept-back crest and wings, red eyes, and striking, multicolored body—are one of nature's most beautiful creatures (and a good reason always to carry binoculars when walking).

The stumps in the water—like the dam—are clues to the lake's history. In the early 1800s, this area was a wet meadow, fed by **natural springs.** The supposed

A fortunate encounter with the striking male wood duck and his mate. They also frequent woodlands near the water's edge.

healing water was bottled and sold, giving the trail its name. After that, the brook was dammed to create a millpond to power a sawmill. However, the dam was lower than today's, so the water level was also lower. When that dam gave way, the water drained, and the area reverted back to a wet meadow again. In 1913, the Lake Shaftsbury Corporation built a larger dam that created the lake here today. As the waters rose, the area to the right of the bridge was flooded and the trees were cut, leaving the stumps. A bungalow colony was then created here for vacationing New Yorkers, billed as "an attractive summer colony for a few people of moderate means."

After that, the area became a Girl Scout camp, and Scouts enjoyed canoeing the open waters west of the bridge. However, nature is always in perpetual transition and lakes are no exception. Silt settles in and leaves fall into the water year after year; **cattails, elephant grass, bulrushes, arrowheads, water lilies,** and trees gradually encroach. This process eventually created the marsh from what had been previously open water. The marsh provides nesting and feeding for birds such as **ducks, green** and **great blue herons, migrating geese, red-winged blackbirds,** and **cedar waxwings** (another of nature's beauties).

Continuing on the esker's ridgeline, look for sprouts of the **American chestnut** tree (there are several along the boardwalk ahead as well). Although chestnuts neared extinction in the 1920s from an Asian fungus, sprouts keep growing from old stumps and root systems. Before they are a dozen feet tall, however, most of them die back from the fungus. Their leaves look very similar to beech leaves, but they are longer and skinnier, and the teeth at the leaves' edges are longer and more pointed.

Reluctantly, we descended from the esker onto a long, beautifully built curving boardwalk over another swampy area, where Warm Brook enters the lake. The boardwalk may be the work of man, but beavers are busy here as well. On the left is a **hornbeam** tree, a tree whose wood is so hard it is sometimes called **ironwood.** A beaver has tried to gnaw it down, first on one side and then on the other, but stopped before completing the job—I suspect because his teeth were simply worn down to the gums. Ten years ago the boardwalk was shorter. When beavers dammed the water on the other side of the railroad tracks, the water seeped through the porous railroad bed and raised the water level on this side so high that another section of boardwalk had to be added. The rangers still contend with beaver construction to keep the boardwalk from being flooded.

The boardwalk provides a good observation point to see the individual stages of **succession** as open water becomes dry land. Looking to the left, the stages are: the **open water** of the lake; nearer the boardwalk is **marsh,** where shallow aquatic plants grow; closer yet is a **shrub swamp;** and on the other side of the bridge is a **tree swamp,** where **red maples** and **hemlock** are growing. The shrub swamp includes **red-osier dogwood,** identifiable by its bright red twigs and stems; **speckled alder,** whose fall fruits look like small pine cones hanging

Patti Mikolas walks the narrow, ridgetop trail atop a 10,000-year-old esker.

from its twigs through the winter; and **bittersweet nightshade,** a vine with purple flowers.

We then curved around the end of the lake, crossed a short boardwalk in a tree swamp, and came to the picnic area. If you visit here in season, pick up a guide to the trail. It is written by Jean E. Vissering (who also illustrated it) and Laura Hollowell. It is one of the finest nature trail guides we have seen. The authors manage to relate the history, topography, and ecology in a seamless description that illuminates one's sense of place as you walk.

How Eskers Form

When mile-thick ice covered this area more than 10,000 years ago, a long crack opened up in the glacier's top as it melted. Water from rain and melted ice ran into the crack and worked its way to the ground under the glacier, where it formed a stream. Over time, as the stream grew larger, it carved an ice tunnel at the bottom of the glacier. At first, the running water carried silt. Then, as its volume and speed increased, it began carrying sand and pebbles. As the mighty glacier melted, more and more water flowed into the stream until it became a small swift river, powerful enough to carry rocks.

The ice tunnel—not the terrain—determined the river's course. But then, after centuries, the ice finally melted away. When it did, this river was no longer confined and immediately changed courses as it sought the lowest ground. When it did, it left behind its old riverbed of rocks and debris that had formed in the ice tunnel. That pile of rubble—the bed of the ancient river beneath the glacier—stands here today as an esker.

Getting There

The entrance to Shaftsbury State Park is located on the east side of Route 7A, 4 miles south of Arlington and 12 miles north of Bennington.

Affiliated Organizations

Vermont Agency of Natural Resources, Department of Forests, Parks and Recreation (Pittsford office).

Canfield-Fisher Memorial Pines

Arlington

- **0.25-mile path, wander among old-growth trees**
- **15–60 minutes**
- **easy**

Towering old-growth eastern white pine, loved and admired by Vermont author Dorothy Canfield Fisher and her family, and left to the state of Vermont in their memory.

If you have never walked through a **virgin forest of eastern white pine,** it might be wise to put it off no longer. It will be 100 years or more before today's large pines begin to reach the size of the trees at Canfield-Fisher Memorial Pines, and the few remaining old-growth stands are disappearing. For example, the September 1938 hurricane blew down stands of virgin pine in both New Hampshire and at Hurricane Forest (page 309). In the late 1980s, a tornado completely destroyed another stand, Cathedral Pines in Cornwall, Connecticut.

Since Europeans first came to our shores, the nature of the forests in the eastern United States has radically changed. Early settlers claimed that a squirrel could travel from the East Coast to the Mississippi River without leaving the crowns of white pines. Pine's value and

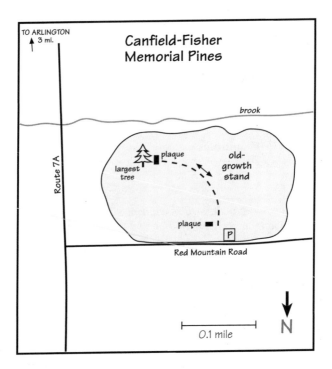

Canfield-Fisher
Memorial Pines

TO ARLINGTON
3 mi.

brook

Route 7A

largest
tree

plaque

old-
growth
stand

plaque

P

Red Mountain Road

0.1 mile

N

usefulness, however, led to their wholesale harvesting. By the end of the 1800s, with only a few exceptions such as this stand, the old growth was gone. Early succession trees moved in to replace them and then eventually gave way to northern hardwoods. Where pines reclaimed the land, their rapid growth led to harvests only 50 years later. Efforts to replant pine forests frequently met with disaster from both the **white pine weevil** and the imported **white pine blister rust**.

In addition to these factors, the need for pasture was so great during the sheep boom that 75 percent of Vermont was cleared of trees 100 years ago. At one time, there were more than a million and a half sheep grazing in Vermont. So much of the land was cleared of trees that **wild turkey, whitetail deer,** and **beaver** all became extinct in Vermont, primarily for lack of habitat. Gazing at these huge trees, one wonders how millions of acres of them could have been decimated by mere axes.

A boulder with a bronze plaque near the trailhead testifies that this area was declared a **Natural Landmark** by the U.S. Department of the Interior. While white pine grows taller than any other tree in the Northeast, don't expect them to be the size of California redwoods. In the northeast, lightning, decay, and wind combine to limit their height to about 140 feet. The tallest tree in Vermont is in East Middlebury at 149 feet. If it were growing at the bottom of Quechee Gorge (page 269), and you looked at it from the Quechee Gorge Bridge, it would fall short of the bridge by about 15 feet. If you've been on the bridge 165 feet above the river, then you realize that that is a pretty tall tree. However, if one of the tallest redwoods were growing at the bottom of the gorge, it would tower 200 feet *above* your head. So hopefully your expectations will not be *too* high—but the Canfield pines are indeed tall trees for the eastern United States. Think of it this way: nearly every other tree you've ever seen in this part of the country is shorter than the first branch of these trees.

We descended on the path that winds through the 13-acre stand and came to one of the largest trees. I

Old-growth eastern white pines with beech understory.

measured it at more than four feet in diameter. There a plaque reads:

Fisher-Scott Memorial Pines, 1975, given to the Vermont Department of Forests in memory of John Redwood Fisher 1883–1959, Dorothy Canfield Fisher 1879–1958, their son, James Canfield Fisher, born December 22, 1913, killed in the Philippines January 31, 1943, their grandson, John Paul Scott, Jr., born October 31, 1943, killed June 6, 1973. All four loved these trees and hills and wanted them preserved in all their natural beauty.

This stand has traditionally been—and continues to be—called the Canfield-Fisher Memorial Pines. The name as it appears on the plaque is not widely recognized. The tree rising above the plaque has heavier branches than the others. Its more dominant crown accounts for its larger growth, but its branches no longer spread wide. The taller trees are the most susceptible to lightning and damaging weather. This giant has stood its ground, resisting the winds, heavy snowfalls, hurricanes, and ice storms for probably far more than 200 winters. The shape of its branches, like the lines in the face of a dear friend growing older, testify to both these trials and its endurance.

The largest tree in the Canfield-Fisher Memorial Pines rises on the right.

Dorothy Canfield Fisher

Dorothy Canfield Fisher, a beloved Vermont writer who lived in Arlington, was a prolific writer. Of her many works, a local favorite is *Vermont Tradition: The Biography of an Outlook on Life,* a history of those who first settled Vermont and their descendants. Through their stories, she reveals the origin of the system of values that distinguishes Vermont from the rest of these United States.

She and her husband were close friends with Norman Rockwell, who lived in Arlington from 1939 to 1953. Rockwell's *Freedom of Speech* poster depicts an

The trees that establish the largest crowns and heaviest branches have the largest diameters.

Arlington Town Meeting. Inspired by those same town Meetings, Canfield Fisher wrote in *Vermont Tradition:* "Vermonters are fiercely unregimented....They will argue with each other and with the Road Commissioner hour after Town Meeting hour, about where to put a culvert." Amen.

Getting There

The pine stand is located along a side road just north of Arlington. From the intersection of Routes 7A and 313 just north of Arlington, proceed north on Route 7A. At 2.3 miles, turn left onto Red Mountain Road. The Memorial Pines are on the left, 0.2 mile up Red Mountain Road. Turn around and pull off on the shoulder at a small opening where the trail leads into the woods.

Affiliated Organizations

Vermont Agency of Natural Resources, Department of Forests, Parks and Recreation (Pittsford office).

In the Area

From the Memorial Pines, it is only a short distance to Manchester and the Pond Loop (page 121) and Boswell Botany Trails (page 128).

If you are interested in old-growth forests, see Gifford Woods (page 188) and Hurricane Forest (page 309).

Branch Pond

Green Mountain National Forest, near Lye Brook Wilderness

- **1.6 miles, level walking on unimproved trails**
- **2–2.5 hours**
- **easy to canoe landing, moderate to pond**

*A walk through wild forest, with several stops
at a small, pristine wilderness pond.*

This is a walk on the wild side. Although the trail into Branch Pond does not take you into the official **Lye Brook Wilderness,** it comes close to its border. The area is meant to be wild and untamed (see Atwood Trail, page 27, where another Congressionally designated wilderness is described).

Two trails leave from opposite sides of the Branch Pond parking lot. The canoe access trail on the left is 0.3 mile long. It was constructed for people carrying canoes and is very easy to walk. At the pond's edge, the clearing is small, providing only enough room for putting in a canoe, but it offers a good view of the southern end of the pond. The clearing farther north on the eastern side of the pond—the Branch Pond Trail destination—is not visible from here. On the right of the landing, we saw a mass of insect-eating **sundews** (see page 279) on a hummock.

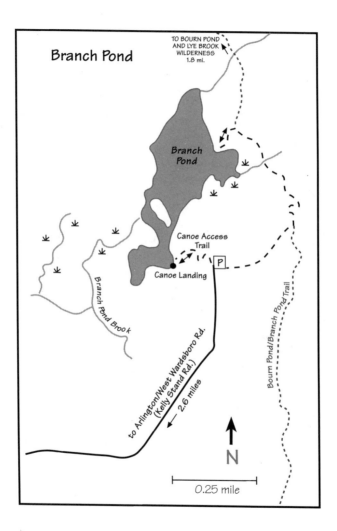

Branch Pond

TO BOURN POND
AND LYE BROOK
WILDERNESS
1.8 mi.

Branch
Pond

Canoe Access
Trail

P

Canoe Landing

Branch Pond Brook

Bourn Pond/Branch Pond Trail

to Arlington/West Wardsboro Rd.
(Kelly Stand Rd.)
← 2.6 miles

N

0.25 mile

From the other side of the parking lot, a spur trail leads to the Bourn Pond/Branch Pond Trail. As you enter the woods on this trail, the world changes from the open parking lot to the hushed silence and darkness of the forest. The trail is obvious in most places, but occasionally it may not be. Keep your eye on the blue blazes, which are more infrequent than those on many trails.

As you approach muddy low spots on the trail, stop to look for footprints. There is a possibility of **moose prints** being spotted. Their prints show a cloven hoof, much like a deer's but far larger; a bull moose print will be the size of your fist or bigger. It is best to have the proper footwear (good hiking boots) and stay on the path. The footing on this trail is that of a forested hiking trail—rocks, roots, leaf litter, and soft spots—and you may have to climb over a blown-down tree or two.

In 0.3 mile, you come to the intersection with the Bourn Pond/Branch Pond Trail. Turn left to Branch Pond. Above you are the gnarled and twisted branches of trees that have battled the weather and competitors for a century or more. Many of the most interestingly shaped trees are **yellow birch,** whose scaly brown bark no longer bears much resemblance to the beautiful golden shine of their youth. Look up, though, and you'll see that the bark of newer high branches is more typical. In the understory of the **paper birch** stands you can see the seedlings and saplings that will overtop them in another generation.

You are in a northern hardwood forest, at about 2,000 feet of elevation. The higher the elevation, the later spring comes and the shorter the growing season.

An old yellow birch sets the character of the trail to Branch Pond.

For every thousand feet of elevation, it's about 10°F cooler. The trees were bare when we walked here in mid-May, while in Vermont's valleys all of the trees except the oaks and locusts had already leafed out. Strangely, some of the wildflowers, like **trout-lily, Indian cucumber-root,** and **false Solomon's-seal,** seemed to be more advanced here than at lower elevations.

The forest floor adds to the sense of untamed nature. The rocky outcroppings on the damp, deeply shaded ground are almost obscured by mosses, ferns, lichen, and small plants. Fallen tree trunks, equally covered by mosses and plants, litter the forest.

A **catbird** sang plaintively from a thicket, and a **veery** hopped about in the brush as we crossed a pond inlet stream on stepping-stones. We paused to savor the small brook's rushing gurgle as it splashed from rock to pool. At a marshy area of the pond to our left, bog-loving plants such as the carnivorous **sundew** and **pitcher-plants** grow on **sphagnum moss** hummocks. However, unless you are prepared for a little bushwhacking and have on rubber boots, these areas around the pond are best explored from a canoe.

At the next trail intersection, a sign indicates Branch Pond 0.1 mile to the left and Bourn Pond 1.8 miles to the right. Bear to the left, and in a short distance is a small pondside clearing. Here we sat, watching the sun set with that wonderful feeling of having left civilization completely behind. The noise of splashing on the pond drew our attention to several pair of **black ducks.** They were washing, cavorting, and chasing one another, splashing water up to catch the low rays of the sun in a golden spray of droplets. A lone **loon** swam about and occasionally dove, popping back to the surface sometimes 60 feet away.

There was no sign of activity from the **beaver lodge** across the water, but before we left, we did see two **osprey** in the distance, having a bedtime snack of fish before flying off to their lofty nests for the night. Other than that, the pond was serene at dusk. We looked for **moose** in the shallow, plant-filled edges of the pond but saw none. The best chance of watching them feed on aquatic plants is at dawn and dusk.

Patti was enraptured with the feeling of primitive remoteness as she listened to birdsongs far and near filling the evening forest. Although this moderate walk deep into the woods is not normally her cup of tea, the fact that it had no uphill climbing and ended at a wonderful destination won her over. On our return in twilight, we flushed out a **ruffed grouse,** sorry to have disturbed it from its repose.

We stopped at a large flat stone bench, placed there with great effort by a trail crew, and sat for a moment in the gathering dusk. I studied the trees growing across the trail. There were two mature paper birches and a yellow birch. All three had very low branches compared with most other trees. To my right were two much older yellow birches leaning westward, and to my left, more distant, another leaning eastward.

Branch Pond on a still evening.

My guess is that the older yellow birch trees are 100 to 150 years old. From their slant, I could see they started life under the canopy of a large tree and had to lean out from under it to find sunlight. The large tree must have been growing in the clearing where the paper birches are now. Judging the distance between the opposite-leaning trees, I could imagine a huge tree with a widely spreading canopy. If so, then it had probably started life at least 200 or 250 years ago and had been either an open-grown or very dominant tree.

Probably 75 to 100 years ago it had been cut and harvested (a natural death would have meant a mound of organic material nearby and there was none). When it was cut, it left a clearing as large as its canopy, letting in enough light for the younger paper birches in front of me to get a start. Their low branches, in turn, show that when they were young, there were no other trees around them shading their lower trunks.

Later, with thanks to Diane Strohm and Laurie Thorpe, rangers for the Green Mountain National Forest, I had a chance to read the management plan for this area. It stated that this land was logged in the early 1900s, when the dominant tree was probably cut. The report also stated that scattered old hardwoods were left. That solved another puzzle: how some of these very aged yellow birch remained in the middle of a forest that was only 80 years old or so.

Under a cobalt sky but in the deepening gloom of the forest, Patti and I walked back to the parking lot. Neither of us spoke, wanting to savor the nighttime silence that was settling down on this primitive world.

How Lye Brook Got Its Name

When the first settlers arrived to clear the land, they knew how to make **potash,** used to make **lye for soap.** They cleared the land, burned the trees, and soaked the ashes in water to produce potash. Primarily because of the great demand for it by large-scale English wool processors, the potash was 10 times more valuable than wheat. That meant that a man could earn a substantial sum by selling only as much as he could pack to market on his back. (A five-ton elm tree produced 39 pounds of potash.) It also compensated him for the huge effort of clearing land by hand.

Then, at the end of the 1700s in France, a less-expensive alkali substitute for lye was discovered. Since the American Revolution had ended only recently, the British were only too happy to turn away from American trade and embrace the new source of raw material. What had been a $1.5 million-per-year Vermont industry in 1810 dropped precipitously to $200,000 three years later, and then to zero. The name Lye Brook, however, lives on.

Birds to Look for in a Northern Hardwood Forest

Two warblers commonly spotted in northern hardwoods have made an interesting adjustment to avoid competition. The **black-throated blue warbler** prefers old, mature forests, while the **American redstart** is more likely to be found in younger, less-mature hardwood forests. Much of Vermont is second growth, with an abundance of young trees, so the redstart—a dark bird whose males are colorfully tinged with orange and females with yellow—is probably Vermont's most common warbler.

While black-throated blue warblers sing from their hidden perches in the understory, the **black-and-white warbler** may be spotted among the trunks of trees. The song of the **red-eyed vireo,** another common bird, keeps repeating monotonously, even when many other birds are silent. Meanwhile, from the understory, the **ovenbird** sings *teaCHER, teaCHER, teaCHER,* rising in volume with each phrase. Its name comes from its dome-shaped nest on the ground, reminiscent of the brick ovens of yore. You may spot the unmistakable red of a **scarlet tanager** perched high in the boughs of the tallest tree around.

The *tutut-eee-o-lay-o-eeee* of the **wood thrush** (identified by its spotted breast and rusty red head) and the *veer veer* of the **veery** seem to best express the joy of being in an undespoiled forest. They are commonly seen on or near the forest floor, where their plumage renders them almost invisible against the dead leaves. The rhythm section of woodland songs is supplied by the drumming of the **pileated, downy,** and **hairy woodpeckers,** joined occasionally, in more open woods, by **northern flickers** and **yellow-bellied sapsuckers.**

When a black, white, and blue streamlined-looking bird is seen climbing down a tree trunk headfirst, it is one of the year-round denizens of the hardwoods: the **white-breasted nuthatch.** Its winter companions include the **blue jay,** the **black-capped chickadee,** and the **hairy woodpecker.**

Bird hawks (*Accipiters*) are the best-equipped hawks to perform the tight flying maneuvers needed to hunt in the forest, sometimes with songbirds as their prey. I watched a brave **robin** attack and drive a **sharp-shinned hawk** away from her nest. He perched till she left and then circled lazily back around, still looking for a quick meal.

I don't have a good ear or good memory for bird-songs, so as they sing from their lofty perches among a million leaves, or flit brown against brown among the underbrush and litter below, I am often at a loss to know who is doing the singing. I solve it by birding by eye in early May, after the songbirds have returned from their Caribbean vacations but before the trees have put out their leaves.

Getting There

Forest Road 70 to the Branch Pond parking lot turns north off the Arlington/West Wardsboro Road (Kelly Stand Road), which is an east/west road that cuts across the Green Mountains. From Route 7A in East Arlington, the turn onto Forest Road 70 is 9.1 miles east on the Arlington/West Wardsboro Road. From the east, the turn is 11.4 miles from Route 100 in West Wardsboro. A large sign marks the turn off the Arlington/West Wardsboro Road onto Forest Road 70. The parking lot is 2.6 miles from the turn, at the end of Forest Road 70. In the winter this road is closed, and the Arlington/West Wardsboro Road may not be passable.

Affiliated Organizations

Green Mountain National Forest.

In the Area

You can plan a longer outing and continue on the trail to beautiful Bourn Pond in the Lye Brook Wilderness. You pass through woods, meadows, and swamp and should be fully prepared with hiking footwear, water bottles, food, etc.

The entrance to Grout Pond is about 5 miles east of Forest Road 70 on the Arlington/West Wardsboro Road. Turn right and a mile-long access road takes you to the park and a beautiful beach on the pond. A 2.7-mile loop trail circles the pond and connects with several other trails, two of which lead south to Somerset Reservoir.

Atwood Trail
Woodford State Park

- **about 0.5 mile (the 2.7-mile Hiking Trail circles the reservoir)**
- **30 minutes**
- **easy**

---

*The Atwood Trail nature walk leads along the Adams
Reservoir, where there is an unusual pondside mix of
vegetation. A more ambitious trail loop passes through
the George Aiken Wilderness.*

A large wetland area lies on the left of the access road
into Woodford. A beaver lodge stands in the middle of
the small pond that formed when it dammed the reservoir outlet stream. A **great blue heron** and **mallards**
were feeding there when we visited.

As you start on the trail, you may notice the sub-
standard quality of the forest. Due to the poor soil conditions and harsh winters, the trees are neither as high
nor as healthy as in most southern Vermont locations.
When the glacier receded 12,000 years ago, it left thick
deposits of **till**—unsorted masses of rocks, sand, and
clay—that make thin, poorly drained soils.

The area is also subjected to the long, harsh Green
Mountain winters. Woodford's elevation, above 2,400
feet, is the boundary between the upper reaches of a

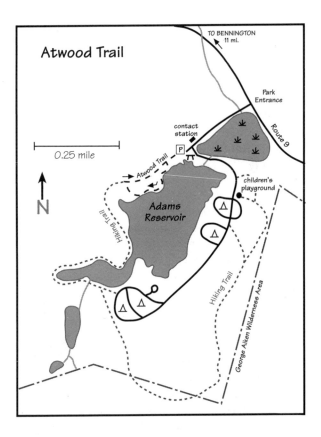

Atwood Trail

TO BENNINGTON
11 mi.

Park
Entrance

Route 9

contact
station

P

0.25 mile

Atwood Trail

N

children's
playground

Adams
Reservoir

Hiking Trail

Hiking Trail

George Aiken Wilderness Area

northern hardwood forest and the lower reaches of a
boreal spruce/fir forest.

We took a left at the first intersection, following the
Nature Trail sign, and walked to the water's edge. I was
surprised to find mats of **sphagnum moss, sedges,** and

leatherleaf (which can be identified by the yellowish cast of the underside of its narrow, toothless, leathery leaves)—and even carnivorous **sundews** (see page 279). I'd expect to see this type of plant life in a bog more than at the edge of a 23-acre lake.

The nature of the reservoir provides a clue. In the early 1800s, Adams Reservoir was created to power sawmills. In 1969, the state rebuilt the spillway, and the water rose, flooding the edges. The rising water killed vegetation around the reservoir, and its incomplete decay created the acidic condition to which bog-type plants are so well adapted.

The trail passes through patches of **hobblebush** (see page 31) and crosses several small brooks. As you walk, keep your ears open for some of the best songsters of the

The Adams Reservoir shoreline, which the Atwood Trail follows.

forests: **warblers** and **thrushes.** After crossing the second brook, the trail turns right and climbs a small hill, where it crosses the brook again on a bridge. Just beyond a bench near the brook, the trail intersects the Hiking Trail. You can turn right on the Atwood Trail and walk back to the parking area, or turn left to start the 2.7-mile Hiking Trail that circles the reservoir and passes through the George Aiken Wilderness for a short distance.

The George Aiken Wilderness

The Atwood Trail traverses terrain typical of the entire 5,060-acre wilderness area: hummocks, bogs, marshes, and small ponds. (The Wilderness Act of 1964 was intended to preserve areas "where the earth and its community of life are untrammeled by man." Thus, other than the one small section of this trail, there are no maintained trails in the Aiken Wilderness, so designated by Congress in 1984.) A trip into the wilderness can provide the solitude and wildness that are in many ways the opposite of park campgrounds and all-too-popular trails. The price to be paid, however, is the challenge of bushwhacking in difficult terrain. Among the rewards are the chance to see **black bear, moose,** and **otters** in their natural habitat and to experience nature on her terms.

George D. Aiken, after whom the wilderness is named, was both a governor of Vermont and an esteemed U.S. senator. He made his home in Putney, where he pioneered wildflower gardening techniques so that flowers growing in the wild would not be picked to extinction (see Boswell Botany Trail, page 132).

Hobblebush

Hobblebush (or **witch hobble**), a *Viburnum*, grows thickly in some places. You're likely to trip over it, because its branches droop until their tips touch the ground, where they promptly reroot. This creates arches, like croquet hoops, and as you catch your foot in them, you'll quickly understand why it is called hobblebush. Its leaves are quite large, dark green, and heart shaped. Its buds are fascinating, suedelike little structures appearing in the very early spring, followed by beautiful clusters of small white or pink flowers.

Hobblebush (witch hobble) buds.

Getting There

Woodford State Park is on the south side of Route 9, about 11 miles east of Bennington. Past the park contact station, continue straight into the picnic area parking lot, where the trailhead is located, rather than following the road, which bears left over the dam.

Affiliated Organizations

Vermont Agency of Natural Resources, Department of Forests, Parks and Recreation (Pittsford office).

Mt. Olga
Molly Stark State Park

- **1.7 miles, 500-foot elevation gain**
- **1.5–2 hours**
- **difficult**
- **bring a jacket, water, binoculars, and camera**

A steep walk to the top of Mt. Olga, where a fire tower offers dramatic 360° views of the mountains of Vermont and Massachusetts.

Molly Stark State Park is at an elevation of 2,000 feet—the average height of the Green Mountains. Even in the summer it can be windy and chilly atop the Mt. Olga fire tower, so you may want to pack a jacket or light sweater.

It is easier to climb a mountain than it is to walk down it, because descending steep slopes is like walking down a ladder while facing outward. Thus, we chose to climb Mt. Olga by the steeper trail and descend on the easier. The trail leaves on the left of the entrance road just after entering the park from Route 9. It passes through shallow, poor soils that support a forest of red maple, white pine, hemlock, spruce, and fir. All of these coniferous species in one place make it ideal to practice differentiating them.

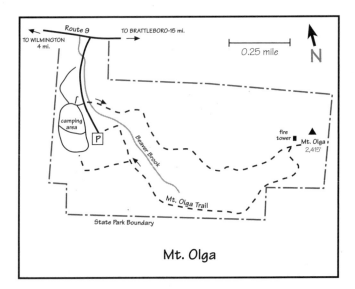

Route 9

TO BRATTLEBORO-15 mi.

TO WILMINGTON
4 mi.

0.25 mile

N

camping
area

P

Beaver Brook

fire
tower ■ ▲ Mt. Olga
2,415'

Mt. Olga Trail

State Park Boundary

Mt. Olga

White pine is recognized easily by its long (two- to three-inch) needles in clusters of five. If the needles of a tree are short, grasp a branch and shake hands with it, remembering the adage: *Spruce is spiky, but fir is friendly.* **Spruce** needles come to a stiff point, and it hurts if you try to grab them. **Balsam fir** needles, on the other hand, are rounded at the end and are much softer. They also give off one of Christmas's most recognizable scents. Although **hemlock** and **fir** look somewhat alike, hemlock needles are much shorter and the tree's twigs are finer. They are fairly easy to distinguish by the leader at the top of the tree—a fir tree points straight up in a coniferous spire, while the top of a hemlock droops lazily (the tips of its branches do the same).

Haystack and Mt. Snow in the Green Mountains, as seen from the Mt. Olga fire tower.

The trail continues upward in a series of short climbs interspersed with more-level walking. We hiked it with a group, and when my wife, Patti, started complaining, the woman in front of her turned around and said, "Well I'm 81 years old." Patti cheerfully continued climbing. When hiking uphill, **set a pace**—no matter how slowly—that allows you to continue talking. If you can talk, then you are getting aerobic exercise; if you can't talk, then it is anaerobic.

At the trail junction near the summit, take a left. Very shortly, we stepped out onto the bare rock of Olga's summit at an elevation of 2,415 feet. A radio relay tower and a fire tower stand here. A wooden fire tower was replaced in 1950 by the steel tower that was reconditioned and moved here from Bald Mountain (page 81). From it, there is a 360° view well worth the trouble of the climb. In Vermont, Harriman Reservoir, Mt. Snow, and Haystack Mountain are visible. To the south lies the Holyoke Range in Massachusetts, and Mt. Greylock can be seen to the southwest.

To return, we descended on the same trail, but bore left at the junction rather than turning right. This trail took us through an area with deep soils. A **sugar maple/beech** forest grows here rather than spruce/fir. However, it was severely defoliated in the early 1980s by an infestation of **saddled prominent moths,** whose

The fire tower on Mt. Olga was moved here from Bald Mountain.

larvae feed on sugar maple and hardwoods, but not ash. There was severe mortality and dieback in the sugar maple, and the dead trees were cut. As a result, **striped maple** moved in. The valley to our right contains the headwaters of Beaver Brook. For a distance, the trail follows an old stone wall, and shortly we reached the campground road.

Who Was Molly Stark?

From 1776 until 1791, Vermont was an independent republic, not a state. In July 1777, even as General John Burgoyne's mighty army was moving toward Hoosick, New York, and Bennington, Vermont, Vermont had no military. In the face of Burgoyne's army, John Chittenden and Ira Allen began forming a ragtag group of volunteers to fight. As they organized, they called upon New York and New Hampshire for assistance.

From New York, General Philip Schuyler sent gunpowder, while New Hampshire's General John Stark led his troops to Bennington to meet Burgoyne. Reports conflict on why Stark's wife, Molly, has become so well known. One account has it that on the eve of the second battle, General Stark said, "Men, there are redcoats. Before night they are ours, or Molly Stark will be a widow." Another account gives Molly credit for assembling additional men in answer to her husband's request and sending them to the battle. Whichever story you prefer, Route 9 from Brattleboro to Bennington is known as the Molly Stark Trail. The Vermonters were victorious in the battle, though at a great loss, and the battle is commemorated by a prominent monument in Bennington.

Getting There

Molly Stark State Park is located on the south side of Route 9 between Wilmington and Marlboro. It is 1.5 miles east of the top of Hogback, where Coomb's Country Market and the Skyline Restaurant are located.

Affiliated Organizations

Vermont Agency of Natural Resources, Department of Forests, Parks and Recreation (North Springfield office).

In the Area

The Luman Nelson Wildlife Museum of Birds and Animals is at Coomb's Country Market, 1.5 miles east of Molly Stark State Park at the crest of the hill. It offers an impressive collection of stuffed mammals and birds (and many oddities). It is well worth an extra half-hour to visit it.

Brattleboro Area

Black Gum Swamp
Vernon

- 0.5–1.5 miles
- 30 minutes–1.5 hours
- easy/moderate

Several rare (in this area) stands of old-age black gum trees growing in swampy depressions. Some individual trees here are 400 years old.

Black gum trees (*Nyssa sylvatica*) are sometimes called **pepperidge** or **sourgum** trees. However, as Donald Culross Peattie writes in his *A Natural History of Trees:* "Nowhere on the American continent has anyone ever expressed from this dry and disobliging vegetable one fluid ounce of any sort of gum. Yet lumbermen and foresters insist on the name." In New England, black gums are also sometimes referred to as **tupelo,** but this confuses them with a different species common in the southern U.S. (as in Tupelo, Mississippi).

Several trails of varying length lead to two different swampy areas. A map of the four trails, their lengths, and the colors with which they are blazed is on the information board at the parking lot, but it is less accu-

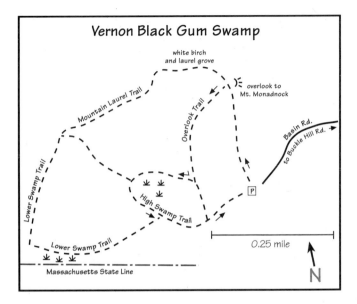

Vernon Black Gum Swamp

rate than the maps available in a mailbox located next to the information board (and reproduced here).

At the parking lot, one sign points to a path on the left, blazed red, that leads to the high swamp in a quarter-mile. It circles the swamp and returns to the parking lot. This trail is rated *easy.* However, if you leave by the right-hand trail, blazed green, it first takes you uphill to an overlook with views to Mt. Monadnock in New Hampshire. Just past the overlook on the left, the green trail leads into the woods. A quarter-mile or so downhill, turn right on the red-blazed trail. Because of the climb and poorer footing, this trail is rated *moderate.*

Centuries-old black gum trees.

Some black gum trees here are 400 or more years old. Black gum is far more predominant in the southern U.S., and it is not really known why such a warm-weather tree is here. One theory holds that it established itself in the north during a warmer period—called the **climatic optimum**—that extended from 5,000 to 3,000 years ago (see page 227 to read how this was determined). When cold weather returned, they all died except for small, relic stands such as this one.

One reason these centuries-old black gum trees were never cut is that their wood fibers are so interlocked that old-timers said it was as easy to split horizontally as it was vertically—meaning it can barely be split at all. Thus, black gum trees were left standing when other, more preferable trees were felled.

The Black Gum Swamp in Vernon has been recognized by the Vermont Natural Resources Council as a **Primary Natural Area,** and its previous owner, architect Jacques Delmarre, sold the land to the town of Vernon in 1973 to preserve them for the public and continuing study. J. Maynard Miller played a key role in educating people about the swamp and preserving the forest. At the 1981 Town Meeting Day in Vernon, it was voted to rename the town forest the "J. Maynard Miller Municipal Forest."

The Vernon Black Gum Swamp is a special place to visit and revisit. In the spring and summer, many varieties of acid-loving wildflowers, ferns, and shrubs (including **highbush blueberry**) can be found in the swamp, and the black gum's seeds attract many birds, such as the **yellow-shafted flicker, wood duck, brown thrush (starling), cedar waxwing, wood thrush,** and **eastern kingbird.** Black Gum's dark-blue, berrylike fruit attracts **fox** and **black bear** as well. The swamp is home to several rare ferns, including the **Virginia chain** and **Massachusetts ferns.** The **aspic puffball** (*Calostoma cinnabarina*), which, like the gum trees, is more commonly a southern species, may be found here. Appearing something like tiny oranges (but stalked and two inches high), they are covered in a gelatinous material. They defy an effective verbal description, but if you hear a child saying, "Yuck. What is that?" — you've probably found them.

Revisit the swamp in September, and you will be rewarded with the blazing dark red of the black gum's leaves, which turn color much earlier than most trees.

How Black Gum Trees Stay Standing in a Swamp

Since black gum often grows in swamps, the trees have a large spreading root mass to hold them upright. However, much of their root systems are only established in peat moss. In high winds, this doesn't always provide a solid-enough anchor for trees that can grow 80 to 100 feet high.

Observe the older black gum trees here and you will see evidence of heart rot in the bottom of their trunks. Although that is common with many trees, black gums have a unique adaptation—they decay so

An ancient black gum whose top has broken off many times.

that their trunks are hollow all the way up into their crowns. As a result, in high winds their tops tend to break off, rather than the entire tree blowing over. This makes black gum the only tree that gets shorter and shorter as it gets older. It also accounts for the scraggly, gnarled look of the upper branches on the larger trees.

Notice too how the bark of older trees is furrowed on the side toward which they lean and smooth on the other side. This strange phenomenon is not fully understood, but one theory holds that snow and ice prevent furrowing on the side exposed to the weather.

Getting There

The Black Gum Swamp is outside of Vernon, about 4 miles south of Brattleboro on Route 142. From the north, turn right off Route 142 onto Pond Road 1.25 miles south of Vernon. You pass immediately under a railroad bridge and continue for 1.2 miles, where you turn right onto Huckle Hill Road. In 1.3 miles, turn right on Basin Road and proceed to its end, which is the parking area for the Black Gum Swamp.

Affiliated Organizations

The Black Gum Swamp is located in the town of Vernon's J. Maynard Miller Municipal Forest.

Sweet Pond
Sweet Pond State Park, Guilford

- 1 mile, fairly level
- 45 minutes (plus lots of time to sit and enjoy it)
- easy

Sweet Pond is just that — a lovely little pond and wetland with perfectly positioned benches for observing birds and waterfowl.

From the parking lot, the trail leads to the right. It is blazed with small blue markers. Sweet Pond was once an estate, and the trail soon leads through a stand of cultivated **Norway spruce.** With a little wind, you can hear them creaking as they sway. As we walked through them and later in the hemlocks, we saw hundreds of branch tips on the ground. The small ones were chewed off by **squirrels,** while larger ones are the work of **porcupines.** Look in the upper branches and you may spot a porcupine gnawing twigs and chewing off bark. Their quills discourage all predators except fishers, so they haven't needed to develop an instinctual fear-or-flight response (see page 147 for a discussion of fishers and porcupines). When I meet a porcupine on the trail, it generally stares at me with mild curiosity, ambles to a tree, slowly climbs to the first branch, sits down, and stares at me some more.

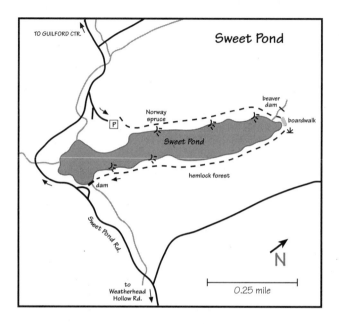

In New York's Catskill Mountains, porcupines have reached nuisance proportions and special precautions are needed. When you park overnight to go camping, the rangers advise that chicken wire be put around the bottom of your car or the porcupines might chew out the gas and brake lines. The quilled critters also have a taste for aluminum. I've seen metal trail blazes chewed down to the nail head and culverts and camp shovels half eaten by porcupines seeking their minimum daily mineral requirements. Wherever hikers grab trees along the trail as handholds, porcupines have girdled the bark; they love that special seasoning of salty perspiration.

Back at Sweet Pond, we soon came to the first of many short spur paths down to the pond's edge. Each leads to a wonderful vista with a hand-hewn bench. From them, we watched for wildlife and waterfowl, listened to the birds, and just enjoyed the tranquillity of the place. As we sat at the first one, we watched a half-dozen pairs of **mallards** swimming and feeding. Back on the trail, just past a stone wall, stood a hemlock on the right that was stitched with horizontal rings of holes, the work of a **yellow-bellied sapsucker.** It is curious how they seem to pick one or two trees and leave all of the others alone. Perhaps the sap is sweeter—but then there appear to be no holes in the surrounding trees, so how would they know?

Zeke Nash takes time out from a mushroom foray at Sweet Pond.

A bench farther along is surrounded by a grove of hemlocks. Most nature experts claim that **beavers** don't like **hemlocks,** but here they've gnawed the bark off the base of several of them. I've seen hemlocks they've girdled that stand right next to paper birch trees. I guess there's just no accounting for taste.

We crossed a small inlet brook on stepping-stones. Nearby were large, **moss-covered stumps,** probably white pine. Because of the pines' resin, their stumps last much longer than one would surmise. Some of the white pines that were blown down in a hurricane nearly 60 years ago still have bark on them, so the stumps here at Sweet Pond could easily be 50 years old or more. There are also a number of dead and dying trees standing in this area. A **flying squirrel** might be nesting in one of their cavities (see next page).

The path continues to another inlet stream, which we again crossed on stepping-stones. A clearing opens on a beautiful view down the pond. This is a good place to watch for birds and waterfowl because your presence can be masked easily by the trees. At the next blazed tree there is another spur to the pond and a bench, set at a scenic spot. As we sat there, the **mallards** we had spotted earlier ran splashing across the water and took off into the air. Ducks that stay north a few days too late in the fall (or if there is an early freeze) can end up sitting in the middle of a pond as the ice closes in. Once there is no longer enough open water for them to use as a "runway," they are trapped.

The beavers have been busy here, and there is a lot of **coppice growth** (sprouted suckers) from tree stumps they gnawed down. At the brook, another trail leads to the left.

This trail is not a park trail, but just a few yards up it is a large **beaver dam.** We then crossed the pond's main inlet on a boardwalk. It is a rich wetland environment of **cattails, speckled alder, ferns, blue-flag irises, horsetail,** and many more marsh plants. Whatever time of year you walk here, there will be something new to see and something new in bloom or going to seed. Even in the dead of winter, the orange berries of the **swamp honeysuckle** and the red branches of the **red-osier dogwood** add color.

Shortly beyond the boardwalk, we spotted a hemlock with tightly knit, foot-long rows of **vertical holes** going up the tree; since **sapsuckers** normally make horizontal rows of holes, this must have been done by one that drills to a different drummer. We then entered a dark forest of old **hemlock.** The **beaver lodge** is visible from here. The trail undulated under the high canopy of evergreens as we stepped silently on the needles. Approaching the southern end of the pond, there were several more benches. Each vista on the trail has been carefully placed to provide a perfect setting, and I'm sure we spent more time sitting and gazing out over this sweet little pond than we did walking around it.

The trail then brings you to the dam, where locals sometimes swim. From the dam, we walked up the road back to the parking lot. We like walking this trail out of season when there are no boats (only oars, paddles, and electric motors permitted) or swimmers, and we can silently appreciate the sweet serenity of the pond.

Flying Squirrels and Natural Cavities
At the north end of Sweet Pond are many trees with cavities created by woodpeckers. Go up to such a tree

and scratch it lightly; sometimes **flying squirrels** will poke their heads out to see what's up. Although seldom observed, both the northern and southern species of flying squirrels are present and very common in Vermont. The slightly larger northern flying squirrel likes coniferous and mixed forests. It appears in the open at deep dusk, and sometimes against the night sky its silhouette can be spotted as it glides from one tree to another lower down, riding the air currents by spreading the webs between its front and back legs.

Flying squirrels are present year-round, though they get more gregarious in the winter, when sometimes 20 or more will den together. Their diet is broader

Does a flying squirrel live here?

than that of red or gray squirrels and includes meat if it's available. During the night, flying squirrels may even glide in to feast at the suet you leave for birds.

Not all of them live in trees; they sometimes build nests on the ground constructed of leaves, twigs, and bark, and they've been known to occupy attics and buildings. To see one, you can sleep out at night under the stars and watch for them against the sky, or do as I do: whenever you see a tree with a cavity in it, scratch it lightly.

Getting There

Sweet Pond, the only state park in southern Vermont with no entrance fee, is southwest of Guilford. Take US 5 south from Brattleboro. Turn right just past the Guilford Country Store onto Guilford Center Road. At 1.7 miles, turn left over the bridge onto Weatherhead Hollow Road. At 4.2 miles, turn right on the unpaved cutoff. Bear right at the top of the hill onto Sweet Pond Road. At 1.7 miles, you see the Sweet Pond dam. At 0.25 mile past the dam, turn right into the state park parking lot.

Affiliated Organizations

Vermont Agency of Natural Resources, Department of Forests, Parks and Recreation (North Springfield office).

In the Area

Not far from Sweet Pond is the Vernon Black Gum Swamp (page 39), a relic stand of 400-year-old black gum trees left here after a warmer period that occurred about 4,000 years ago.

Fort Dummer State Park
Brattleboro

- 1.5 miles total
- Sunrise Trail 45–50 minutes, Sunset Trail 10–15 minutes
- easy

A walk through a forest more typical of areas south of here offers a view of the Connecticut River Valley where Fort Dummer used to stand. A path leads through a steep cut into an old slate quarry.

At the end of the paved park access road, where it joins the two camping loop roads, a sign points straight ahead for the Sunrise Trail. We soon came to the Connector Trail, which provides a shortcut to the vista, but we turned left at the first intersection to walk the full loop. Walking here, we saw a **hermit thrush** (page 57), Vermont's state bird. A boardwalk leads to a hemlock forest and a softly needled path, marred only by the **excessive blazing** of the trail. Farther on, an identification plaque for **red maple** (*Acer rubrum*) is on the left. It is also known as **scarlet maple** or, because of its affinity for low, wet areas, **swamp maple.** There is something red on the tree year-round: in summer, the stems and emerging leaves of new growth; in the fall, its leaves turn red; in winter it's buds and twigs; and

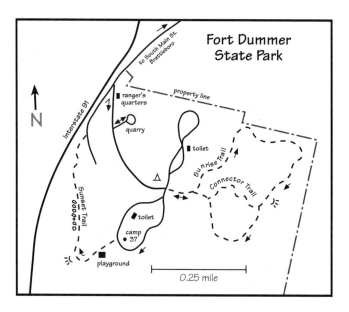

Fort Dummer
State Park

N

Interstate 91

to South Main St.
Brattleboro

property line

ranger's
quarters

quarry

toilet

Sunrise Trail

Connector Trail

Sunset Trail

△

toilet

camp
37

playground

0.25 mile

in spring, its clusters of small flowers that hang from the branches.

The red maple is also known as **soft maple,** distinguishing it from the state tree of Vermont, the **sugar** or **hard maple.** There are several ways to tell the trees apart. The leaf sinuses (the indentations between the lobes) of a sugar maple are U-shaped. Those of a red maple are V-shaped (think of sUgar and Vermilion). On older trees, the plates of bark on the soft maple can be easily pried off, while if you try to do that with a hard maple, your fingernails are liable to go first. Red maple bark often breaks up into round bull's-eye patterns,

Bull's-eye bark patterns typical of red maple.

which stand out clearly as you glance through a stand of trees. This pattern is an instant and certain identification.

The woods then become dominated by **white, red, and chestnut oak**—more like a forest in southern New England than in Vermont. **Wintergreen** and **princess pine** (a **clubmoss**) love the acid soil of decayed oak leaves—and they often cover the floor of an oak forest. Look also for **chestnut sprouts** along the trail. Their leaves are similar to beech but are longer, thinner, and the serrations come to a more pronounced point. **Sassafras trees** can be spotted by their unusual leaves (see page 62).

We crossed a second boardwalk and came to a bench at the vista. The view is to the southeast, giving rise to the Sunrise Trail's name. Before us was the Connecticut River, broadened by the water backed up behind the Vernon Dam. **Fort Dummer,** built in 1724 on the river's bank, was the first permanent white settlement in Vermont. It provided a frontier gateway for new settlers coming north along the Connecticut River and later protected what was then a Massachusetts colony from invasion during the French and Indian War. When the Vernon Dam was built in 1908, the site of the fort was flooded. In the devastating **March 1936 flood**—when the region was deluged by rain that melted the deep remaining snow cover—streams rose 16 feet above their normal levels. Water up to 11 feet deep cascaded over the Vernon Dam, but it held. If it hadn't, Greenfield, Massachusetts, would have been washed away.

Shortly beyond the vista, you can cut directly back to the campground on the Connector Trail. We continued on the Sunrise Trail, where we soon saw a true **flowering dogwood** on the left. It blooms from April to June with two- to four-inch white flowers whose four petals are notched at their tips. Technically speaking, however, these are not the flower's petals; they are **bracts,** designed to lure insects into the heart of the bloom, where they pollinate the small, inconspicuous greenish-white flower. If the dogwoods are not in bloom, look for purple twigs. Most dogwoods found growing wild in forests are not of this variety and do not have the showy flowering of the *Cornus florida.*

Soon the Sunrise Trail joins the Connector Trail, and together they arrive back at the trailhead. There, turn left on the campground road to proceed to the Sunset Trail. Near Camp 37, a pathway leads left across an open playground. Cut straight across staying to your left and in a few steps you are on a high bluff looking west over I-91. If it weren't for I-91, this would be a postcard view of the rolling green hills of Vermont checkered with meadows and farm fields. There's even a white church steeple in Guilford. Oh well—at least the highway makes it easier to get here than it was for the settlers who arrived by ox- or horse-drawn cart.

The trail then descends down close to I-91, where there are both **American** and **slippery elm** trees on the left. With their rough bark, slippery elms do not look slippery; they are named after their slippery inner bark, which is also the source of slippery elm lozenges, used to quell coughs. On the right is a stand of white pine, but nearly all of them are **cabbage pine** (**wolf trees** or **candelabra trees**)—those whose top leader was killed by the **white pine weevil.** The side shoots then formed leaders, creating misshapen trees that no longer have commercial value as sawlogs.

Turn left on the paved road and return to the park entrance. Walk up the entrance road past the ranger station and on your left you will see a mound of tailings from an old **slate quarry.** Just past this mound, an unmarked trail to the left leads through a beautiful cut in the stone into the quarry. The quarry itself is 80 feet deep, about 75 feet long, and 35 feet wide. The walls rise high on all sides, their height accentuated by the vertical veins of shale. It is filled with about 40 feet of

The author at the entrance to the Fort Dummer quarry.

water. As local legend has it, an old farmer who once owned the property disappeared one night on his aging white horse. It is said that they fell together into the quarry pond.

Vermont's Hermit Thrush

A **hermit thrush** is sometimes nicknamed (along with its brother, the **wood thrush**) the **swamp angel** or **swamp robin.** It is a little larger than a sparrow, with a brown back, a speckled breast, and a **rufous tail,** easily spotted in flight. Its habit of cocking its tail up and then lowering it again slowly distinguishes it from the similar **veery** and **wood thrush.**

It prefers thickets and cool woods, where it breeds and, with its coloring, disappears easily against the understory and leaf litter. Its eggs are a light blue. The thrushes are related to the nightingale, and their songs — heard most often at twilight — are among the most beautiful in the forest. The hermit thrush's song is usually described as "ethereal" or "flutelike." To me, both its song and that of the veery sound like running one's mouth back and forth across a bamboo panpipe. Unlike the veery and wood thrush, the song of the hermit thrush always begins with a **long single note,** as if to announce, "Listen up. I'm about to sing."

Charles Johnson, Vermont state naturalist, has noted that the thrushes seem to establish their homes at differing altitudes. The **gray-cheeked thrush** is predominant near the tree line in spruce/fir forests; **Swainson's thrush** is heard lower on the mountainside; the **hermit thrush** is found in the mixed woods below that; and the **wood thrush** farther below in hardwood forests.

Getting There

From Exit 1 on I-91 heading toward Brattleboro on US 5 (Canal Street), turn right at the first light onto Fairground Road. Pass the high school on the right. At the stop sign, take a right on South Main Street. The street name changes to Old Guilford Road. Continue and it ends at the state park entrance.

Affiliated Organizations

Vermont Agency of Natural Resources, Department of Forests, Parks and Recreation (North Springfield office).

Wantastiquet Mountain
Hinsdale, New Hampshire

- **1.4-mile round-trip, 1,100-foot elevation gain**
- **2–3 hours**
- **difficult**
- **bring camera, binoculars, and good walking shoes**

Brattleboro's most well known hike leads to a perspective from which many of southern Vermont's geologic features are clearly visible.

Although Wantastiquet Mountain is in New Hampshire, the trailhead lies just over the Connecticut River from Brattleboro, and the views it affords are all to the west, into Vermont. Native Americans called the West River **Wantastiquet,** meaning "waters that flow from the west." The West River joins the Connecticut River at the base of the mountain, and the Retreat Meadows at their confluence is clearly visible from its summit. There are few people living in Brattleboro who haven't climbed Wantastiquet. Visiting Brattleboro in 1856, Henry David Thoreau wrote in his journal: "Above all, this everlasting mountain is forever lowering over the village, shortening the day and wearing a misty cap each morning. You look up to its top at a steep angle from the village streets."

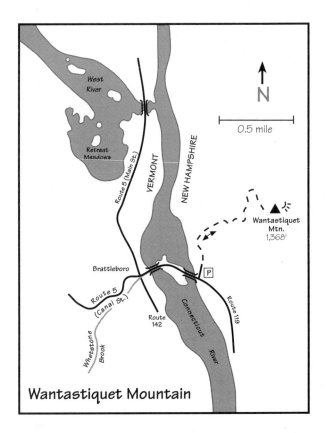

Wantastiquet Mountain

Everywhere else in the United States, state borders occur in the middle of rivers that divide them. However, after more than a century of border disputes between Vermont and New Hampshire, the U.S. Supreme Court ruled in 1933 that the New Hampshire

Brattleboro lies at the foot of Wantastiquet on the Connecticut River, with the Green Mountains on the horizon.

border extends to the low-water mark on the western (Vermont) side of the river. Thus, the Connecticut River is all in New Hampshire—unless it floods.

The trailhead is marked by an iron gate and stone post inscribed Wantastiquet Road. The trail, with its series of nine switchbacks, was once used as a road to the mountaintop and nearby quarries. Wantastiquet's summit is actually an extended series of multiple peaks and ledges where **ocher** was once mined. The trail is broad, unblazed, and eroded, like most old mountain roads.

We classify this trail *difficult* in relation to other nature trails. For hikers, it may be a breeze, but to someone who is used to walking several level miles on easy paths, it will be a bit of a challenge. We recommend that you wear hiking boots and set an easy pace. Take your time to look around and watch subtle changes in the forest and understory as you climb.

Look for young **sassafras** saplings along the trail. Their leaves may be any of three different shapes: plain ovate, two-lobed, or three-lobed. The two-lobed shape is often referred to as *mittenlike,* while the handsome three-lobed leaves remind me of a first-baseman's mitt. The leaves of other deciduous trees, like northern red oak, can also take a variety of shapes as a result of factors like age, nutrition, and sunlight. It can make tree identification by leaf shape difficult. Like black and yellow birch and black cherry, smell can be used to aid in

On this sassafras seedling, all three of its leaf shapes appear together.

identifying sassafras. Its aromatic bark and roots were once used to flavor root beer and are still used to perfume soap and to make sassafras tea. I love the intense aroma of a crushed leaf.

Birds you might see on this walk include the **cerulean warbler, rufous-sided towhee, scarlet tanager, ovenbird, black-and-white warbler, northern oriole,** and several varieties of **thrushes.**

You'll also see **mountain laurel** along the trail. Its stiff leaves are present year-round, so it adds a friendly green border to the trail, even in snowbound winter. Many locals hike Wantastiquet in May and June just to enjoy the display of the mountain laurel's large pink

When a bee lands on a mountain laurel bloom, it triggers the anthers—attached at the 10 dark spots—which then spring up, spraying its legs with pollen.

and white clusters of blossoms. Because it is an acid-loving plant, its presence here—in the Granite State—is one of the first clues that the geologic makeup of south-western New Hampshire is quite distinct from that of Vermont.

Our destination was marked by a checkerboard-painted granite marker in a clearing to the right. It is surrounded by open rock and made a fine place to rest after our climb. From it, we enjoyed the reward of a broad view of Brattleboro and the Connecticut and West River valleys. To the west are the undulating hills that stretch all the way to Vermont's spine: the Green Mountains—a perspective from which one can appreciate the larger features of the land in which many of the walks in this book are located.

After resting and enjoying the view (and following the soaring and gliding of a **red-tailed hawk** with our binoculars), we descended on the same trail.

A Geologic Perspective from Wantastiquet Mountain

Over several hundred million years, land forms stretched and broke apart and collided into one another, forming today's continents and oceans. Geologists have determined that Wantastiquet was once part of a chain of ocean islands, the **Bronson Hill Island Arc.** It was compressed against North America when Europe and Africa collided with our continent. In fact, eastern parts of Maine, New Hampshire, and Massachusetts are parts of Europe or Africa that stuck to North America when the continents drifted apart again.

The Bronson Hill Island Arc was a series of **domes** created when plugs of magma pushed up underground and cooled very slowly, becoming **granite** (to read how granite forms, see Black Mountain, page 73). Granite creates acidic soils, which is why mountain laurel, which grows only in acidic soils, is found along the Wantastiquet trail. The geology of southeastern Vermont is completely different from that of Wantastiquet, and as a result, very little mountain laurel grows there.

When people drive north on I-91 from Massachusetts, they often remark that "somehow" it feels different when they enter Vermont. There are some cultural reasons for this—for example, Vermont has no roadside billboards—but another good reason is that in Connecticut and Massachusetts, I-91 follows a geologic region known as the **Connecticut Valley Lowland.** This ends abruptly at the Vermont border; as you enter Vermont, you climb onto a plateau, or **piedmont,** which slopes eastward to the ocean and from which the various Vermont and New Hampshire mountains rise.

From Wantastiquet, you can observe that the rolling hills across eastern Vermont are all roughly the same height, defining the level of what was once a **peneplain** as flat as the Great Plains. The landscape and topography you see today has been carved out of that plain by ice and water and is now in what geologists call the **mature stage of stream erosion.** The Green Mountains in the far distance are actually part of a formation that extends southward down the eastern coast of the U.S. and includes the Blue Ridge Mountains. Between the Green Mountains and New York

State lies another separate, smaller ridge of mountains—the Taconics, whose presence remains a geologic mystery (page 118).

During the Ice Age, all of this land, including where you are standing, was covered several times by massive **glaciers**—a mile or more thick. About 14,000 years ago, as the last one melted northward, a valley in Rocky Hill, Connecticut, became dammed with debris. As a result, water backed up behind the natural dam and formed a 200-mile-long lake that stretched from south of Hartford, Connecticut, to Vermont's Northeast Kingdom. **Glacial Lake Hitchcock,** as it is now called, filled the valleys of the Connecticut River and its tributaries. In Brattleboro, its level reached to just behind the Brattleboro Memorial Hospital (on Canal Street just east of I-91 Exit 1). Evidence in clays and soils makes it possible to accurately map the lake's ancient shoreline. At the Allard sandpit on Old Ferry Road, near the Brattleboro landfill, the lake's shore was found to be more than *30 feet higher* than it had been at the hospital.

How could a lake's shoreline slope uphill? Obviously it couldn't, but geologists reason that as the glacier melted away, the land that had been compressed by the enormous weight of thousands of feet of ice actually sprang back, like a mattress does when you get out of bed (only far more slowly). Since the ice was thicker and heavier to the north, the more northern the land, the more it was compressed—and the higher it sprang back. Lake Hitchcock's shoreline rises progressively higher all the way up the Connecticut River Valley—

illustrating one of the many effects glaciers have had in shaping the land.

Observe the sides of the valley following the Connecticut River and you will notice that the land rises away from the water in a series of terraces. These define the different levels of floodplains as Lake Hitchcock drained away to the south. Brattleboro is actually built on such a terrace, and throughout Vermont's river valleys, many such terraces are the sites of productive farms.

Getting There

As Thoreau said, Wantastiquet rises above Brattleboro just across the Connecticut River in New Hampshire. From the intersection of Main and Canal streets, Bridge Street leads across the river. Immediately after the second bridge, turn left onto a dirt road, which shortly terminates at the trailhead, where parking is provided.

In the Area

If you'd like to get closer to the river, you can rent a canoe at Connecticut River Safari (located at the cove at the West River Bridge on Putney Road, 802-254-3908). From there, you can paddle the still waters of the Retreat Meadows, a wetland formed at the mouth of the West River. The Meadows is an excellent area for waterfowl and bird-watching, often offering unusual surprises.

Black Mountain
Dummerston

- 1.5-mile round-trip, 235-foot elevation gain
- 2 hours
- moderate (uphill but easy walking)

Observe a fascinating change in ecology, see evidence of hand-quarried granite, and enjoy great views to the south-east — all with a relatively short climb.

The trail to this summit of Black Mountain (which has several summits) is an old road that is easy to walk. Enter the gate at the trailhead and proceed through a recently thinned oak/sugar maple forest. Within a few minutes, you arrive at what looks like a broad natural amphitheater on the left. As you stand at its base, observe that the tops of the trees growing around you are virtually even with the tops of the much shorter trees that grow from the top of the ridge. Where you are standing, the soil is derived from the underlying mica schist rock with limestone. Trees love the relatively alkaline diet provided by this type of soil and grow well in it. The soil on the ridge, on the other hand, is shallow and acidic as a result of the granite bedrock that forms the ridge. The stunted ridgetop trees reflect this difference by growing much more slowly.

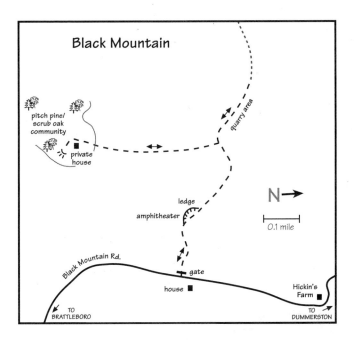

Black Mountain

pitch pine/
scrub oak
community

private
house

ledge

amphitheater

quarry area

Black Mountain Rd.

gate

house

Hickin's
Farm

N→

0.1 mile

TO
BRATTLEBORO

TO
DUMMERSTON

At the top of the ridge, the trail you are on continues straight, but take a left to the peak. When we last walked it, the sun had just begun to burn through the morning's fog and its rays filtered from the east through the mist and pines—a rare and memorable moment that makes one ask, "Why don't we do this more often?"

As you approach the summit, you can spot three different kinds of pine trees native to Vermont: **white pine,** with its long soft needles in clusters of five; **pitch**

pine, with three shorter needles in a cluster; and **red pine,** with two prickly needles. It is easy to identify pitch pines, because they are the only ones whose needles grow out of the bark of its trunk and branches.

Soon you emerge from the pines onto open granite ledges with views to the southeast. (The small house here is private, as is the land. Enjoy the views, but do not disturb the house. No camping or fires are permitted.) Because of its granite-created acidic soils, the ecology of Black Mountain's peak is unique in Vermont. Here the white, red, and pitch pines are joined by other acidic loving shrubs—**mountain laurel, blueberries, and scrub oak.** Scrub oak is found nowhere else in Vermont. As a result, Black Mountain's summit appears

Scrub oak and pitch pine grow from the granite top of Black Mountain. Wantastiquet Mountain rises in the distance.

much like the terrain of Cape Cod or the New Jersey Pine Barrens.

Along the path and on the ledges, observe the crescent-shaped depressions in the stone—these are **crescentic fractures.** They are formed by rocks digging into the granite under the massive weight of the glacier. As the ice flowed over the granite, rocks would be picked up, carried a little farther, and then dropped to dig in again. Look around this area and you will find crescentic fractures of many different sizes. A series of them usually appears in a line, which provides a rock-engraved record of the **glacier's direction of travel.** Distant but similar fractures running in about the same direction as these can be seen at White Rocks (page 157).

Crescentic fractures in the granite indicate the direction of the last glacier's movement.

When ready to leave, return on the same trail to the T intersection. If you take a right, you return the way you came. Take the left, however, and the road continues downhill on the northwest side of the mountain and curves to the right. In about five minutes, you will see a large slope of granite rubble on the hillside to your right. Walk among the rocks here and look for signs of early quarrying. You will find drill and chisel marks on many of the granite slabs.

The remains of a large, successful **granite quarry** lie at the foot of Black Mountain on the West River. A piece of granite from that quarry is in the Washington Monument. But men climbed up here to quarry and dress granite by hand for their own needs. They made such items as lintels, doorsteps, and granite fence posts. In the slow winter months, farmers would quarry and dress granite to sell for additional income. As you climb over the rubble looking for traces of their work, look for at least two nearly finished **millstones** — about four feet in diameter and hewn by hand out of the mountain.

As I retraced my steps back to the car, I visualized these men who climbed the mountain each day, tools in hand, to work at shaping stone. Listen quietly and you can still hear the ring of their hammers on cold chisels, the grate of steel pry bars on rock, and the laughter and conversation among them as they worked, occasionally coming together to help someone shift a large chunk of granite. Why, I still wonder, did the two men who were working on the millstones give up so close to being done?

How Granite Forms

Nearly 400 million years ago and miles underground, deep ocean sediments were folded over on themselves and became **mica schist,** a **sedimentary rock.** Erosion began slowly wearing away the miles of earth's surface above it. At about the same time, a **dome of magma** (molten lava) pushed its way up into the schist and started to cool, crystallizing into **granite.** From its molecular structure, it can be determined how rapidly or slowly it cooled, and from that, how far under the earth it formed. The crystalline structure of the granite here indicates that Black Mountain formed originally about 12 miles under the earth.

Millions of years of erosion and glacial action wore down these miles of earth, finally reaching the level of the granite. Since it was harder than the surrounding

A granite millstone hand-hewn from the bedrock.

mica schist, it eroded much more slowly than the surrounding rock, leaving what we know today as Black Mountain standing above its surrounding valleys.

Getting There

Black Mountain rises from the eastern side of the West River in Dummerston. From Dummerston Center, go west on the East-West Road toward West Dummerston. In about 1.0 mile, you will see a sign for Hickin's Picking Farm. Turn left on Black Mountain Road. The road bears right at Hickin's farm. The trailhead is on the right, just past a large white house on the left. Look for a gate blocking access to a woods road — this is the trailhead. Park along the road and close the gate behind you as you begin and end your walk.

Affiliated Organizations

Much of the land on Black Mountain is Nature Conservancy land. However, the summit is private land, and the owner — kind enough to permit the public to enjoy this beautiful spot — asks that you respect the land and the cottage there. You are requested specifically not to build fires or camp.

In the Area

To visit the remains of the large commercial Black Mountain quarry, return to the East-West Road and take a left toward West Dummerston. Turn left on Quarry Road at the foot of the hill just before the covered bridge. The quarry is on your left, about a mile down Quarry Road, which follows the river.

Putney Mountain
Putney

- 1-mile round-trip, 140-foot elevation gain
- 1 hour (allow additional time to spend on top)
- easy
- binoculars for hawk watching

*An easy walk with spectacular views of the Green
Mountains and Grand Monadnock. In late September,
it is a superb place to observe migrating hawks.*

There are Vermont mountains—like Mts. Ascutney,
Mansfield, and Equinox—where one can drive a car to
the summit and enjoy the views, but most mountain
summits are enjoyed only by ambitious hikers who find
pleasure in walking uphill. Putney Mountain is a combination of both: one drives most of the ascent, and
then, with an easy and enjoyable half-mile walk
through the woods, is rewarded by a spectacular
panorama from the mountain's summit.

The first stop, 15 minutes up the trail, is always at
what kids call the **Elephant Tree.** Only several feet off the
ground, a branch—two feet or more in diameter—veers
straight out eight feet from the massive trunk of this
ancient **white ash,** and then veers suddenly upward, like
a giant showing off the gnarled biceps of his arm. Native
Americans once bent saplings as trail markers, and some
think that accounts for the tree's unusual shape.

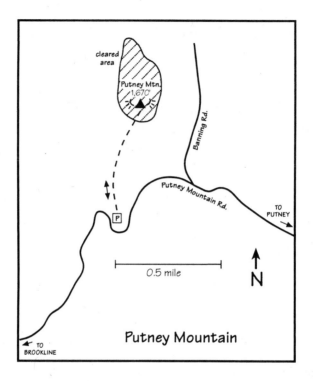

cleared area

Putney Mtn.
1,670'

Banning Rd.

Putney Mountain Rd.

TO PUTNEY

P

0.5 mile

N

TO BROOKLINE

Putney Mountain

The trail ascends gently and changes from earth to outcropped rock; tall woodland trees give way to their smaller, struggling brothers on the thin soils near the exposed summit. Soon you emerge onto the mountain's rocky summit, at an elevation of about 1,670 feet. To the east is **Grand Monadnock,** as Mt. Monadnock is known locally. It is the second most-climbed peak in the world (Mt. Fuji in Japan is the first). Its name is used by geolo-

The "elephant tree," a favorite of children on the trail to the top of Putney Mountain.

gists to describe mountains that stand alone above a peneplain. Mt. Ascutney, another nearby monadnock, is discussed in Springweather (page 238). On the western side, we could see the **Green Mountains.** Starting from the south, look for ski trails to identify Haystack, Mt. Snow, Stratton, and (when the foliage is off the trees) Bromley.

Prevailing winds blow from the west, and as they hit the Putney Mountain ridge they create **updrafts.** If you visit in late September and bring binoculars, you can join the many birders who come to count **migrating hawks.** The hawks take advantage of the updrafts by flying down the ridgeline. Many varieties—along with the occasional **bald eagle** and **osprey** (fish hawk)—are spotted. These large raptors are diurnal; they fly south only during daylight. To avoid them, many smaller species of migratory birds have evolved to fly only at night.

To leave, return by retracing your steps back to the parking area.

How Nature Shaped Putney Mountain

What began as mud at the bottom of a deep sea hundreds of millions of years ago was compressed by a land mass colliding with North America (see Prospect Rock). The mud folded upward like an accordion, and — under intense heat and pressure — became **schist.** On the eastern side of Putney's peak, you can see shiny flecks in the schist. This variation is called **mica schist.** The pea-sized bumps in the surface of some of the stones contain tiny **red garnets.** A different kind of bedrock — a black form of schist called **amphibolite** — makes up the western side. It was formed at the bottom of the ancient sea through volcanic activity and was folded upward with the mud.

The land mass that ran into North America did so from the east, so the folds it formed — like the Putney Mountain ridge — run north-south. The ridge is rock that contains more hard **quartz** than surrounding formations. Thus, the land around the mountain has eroded away more rapidly, leaving Putney Mountain.

Notice Mt. Monadnock's profile in the far distance: a long sloping ridge from the north leads to the top, while the mountain falls off to the south more sharply from the summit. You experience this difference hiking on Monadnock. While the Pumpelly Trail climbs four

East from Putney Mountain, New Hampshire's Grand Monadnock rises in the hazy distance.

and a half miles on its northern slope to the summit, the trails that originate in the state park on its southern side climb far more steeply for about half the distance.

Putney Mountain has this same characteristic shape; its northern slope is relatively gradual when compared with its southern face, which drops off more precipitously. In fact, most of Vermont's mountains—Ascutney, Black Mountain (page 68), and many of the Green Mountains and Taconics—have similar profiles. All of them were shaped by the last glacier. As it moved south, it passed over the northern sides of mountains scouring them smooth. It then passed over their tops, ripping away fragments of rock and scattering them southward as erratics.

Getting There

Putney Mountain is located in Putney, 10 miles north of Brattleboro. From I-91 Exit 4, turn left to the center of Putney. At the Putney General Store, turn left onto Westminster West Road. At 1.1 miles, turn left onto West Hill Road. Bear right as you pass Houghton Brook Road. At Aiken Road, bear sharply left, staying on West Hill Road. Shortly beyond Aiken Road, Holland Hill Road and Putney Mountain Road are on the right. Turn right and bear right onto the unpaved Putney Mountain Road. In 2.1 miles, as you reach the crest of the mountain, the parking lot for the summit walk is on the right. At the end of the parking area, the footpath begins slightly uphill (do not take the old woods road that heads downhill to the right).

Affiliated Organizations

The parking lot and much of the Putney Mountain trail are part of the Putney Town Forest. The summit is owned by the Putney Mountain Association, a private organization whose volunteer members maintain the trail.

In the Area

For wildflower lovers, a visit to the Putney Nursery, just south of the village center on US 5, is in order. The nursery was founded and operated for many years by Putney resident George D. Aiken. To read more about Aiken and his political career and avocation of collecting, studying, and growing wildflowers, see page 132.

Bald Mountain
Townshend State Park

- **3.4-mile round-trip; 1,100-foot elevation gain (or less if preferred)**
- **1–3 hours (depending on destination)**
- **moderate/difficult**

A moderate walk along a brook passes a tree identification quiz. A more difficult climb brings you to an alder swamp, and a final short but steep ascent brings you to the summit and its views.

Bald Mountain is located in Townshend State Park, which in turn is in the Townshend State Forest. Acquired in 1912, the 856-acre forest is one of the state's oldest landholdings. The eastern ascent of this loop trail is very steep and can be slippery. Thus, you may want to both ascend and descend on the slightly longer but easier western side of the loop. From the park office, a spur trail leads down the bank to the right and crosses a pole bridge. Turn left and follow the brook upstream on the blue-blazed trail. Along the trail, there are a number of trees with small signs in front of them that show a question mark. Guess the **tree's identity,** and then lift the hinged top to see if you are right.

Unfortunately, at the time of this writing, there are three misidentified trees and one misspelling. These will probably have been corrected by publication or removed,

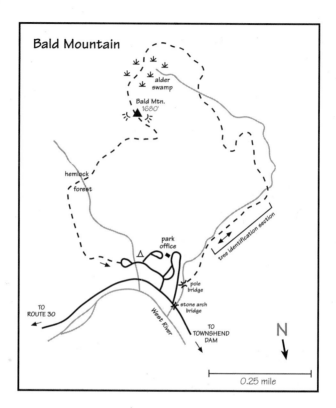

Bald Mountain

alder swamp

Bald Mtn.
1680'

hemlock forest

park office

tree identification section

pole bridge

stone arch bridge

West River

TO ROUTE 30

TO TOWNSHEND DAM

N

0.25 mile

but if not, see if you can find the two **black birches** that are marked as a **cherry** and as a **gray birch,** and the **striped maple** marked as a **mountain maple** (see page 84).

The walk up the old road along the cascading brook is a very pleasant one, and for those who want to take it easy, turn around at any point to return. If you continue, the trail cuts left back across the brook and climbs upward on several switchbacks. Windham County Forester Bill Guenther made the elevation measurements of the area and he also made and erected signs that mark each 200 feet of **elevation gain** on the trail. Use these signs to acquire an experience of how much climbing 200 feet represents.

At just over a mile from the beginning of the trail, you come to an **alder swamp** on the right. From here, it is a short distance and about a 300-foot climb to the summit of Bald Mountain (elev. 1,680 feet). A wooden fire tower was originally built there in 1924. During the Great Depression, a Civilian Conservation Corps (CCC) camp based here replaced the tower with one of steel. To see the steel tower, climb Mt. Olga (page 33), since it was subsequently renovated and moved there.

Bald Mountain on the right, as seen from the top of Townshend Dam.

Looking from Bald Mountain to the east and southeast, you see Mt. Monadnock in New Hampshire and the West River Valley below you. To the northwest are Stratton and Bromley mountains. When ready to leave the summit, you can head north to take the steeper easterly loop or return the way you came.

Distinguishing Trees at Bald Mountain

The **black birch** is one of the trees that can be identified with your nose. Break a small twig or roll a leaf between your fingers and its strong scent of wintergreen cannot be mistaken. Its sister tree, the **yellow birch,** has a similar aroma. The black birch's dark bark forms large vertical plates as it grows older. It is very easy to distinguish it from **black cherry,** whose bark makes the tree look as if it were covered with **burnt potato chips.** Once you've seen and positively identified a cherry, you'll never confuse it with a black birch again.

Striped maple goes by many names: **striped maple,** from its white-on-green striped bark; **goosefoot maple,** after the shape of its large leaves; **moosewood,** a common nickname for many different trees browsed by moose; and **whistlewood,** because its bark slips off in the spring, the first step in making a wooden whistle. In Boy Scouts, we were taught to call it **camper's toilet paper,** and its very large, pliable leaves have served me well ever since. Woodlot owners call it a **weed,** because it grows fast, has little value, and crowds out more desirable trees. The bark of **mountain maple** has no stripe, so it shouldn't be confused with striped maple.

The distinctive "burnt potato chip" look of black cherry bark.

Horizontal white lenticels—the speckles that give **speckled alder** its name—cover the dark bark. It is usually shrub size and grows in wet thickets. Its double-toothed leaves look much like those of ironwood and hornbeam, but are rounder. Its fruit looks like small cones that remain on its branches through the winter.

Woodcock and **grouse** find alder an especially desirable habitat. Grouse feed on its buds, while **muskrat, hare, deer,** and **moose** browse its twigs. Of all the trees available to them, speckled alder is the most preferred by nine out of 10 beavers.

The alders provide a good case for referring to trees by their scientific Latin names; while **speckled alder** (*Alnus rugosa*) is sometimes called **black alder,** there is a different species (*Alnus glutinosa*) known as **European black alder.** To confuse matters further, a completely unrelated shrub, **common winterberry holly** (*Ilex verticillata*) is also called **black alder.**

Getting There

Two miles northwest of Townshend Village on Route 30, take a left and cross the Townshend Dam on the narrow road. (As you cross the dam, look to your left for a good view of **Bald Mountain**). When the road comes to a T, turn left. In 0.6 mile, bear right at the **Scott Covered Bridge.** Continue another 0.6 mile to the park entrance on the right.

Affiliated Organizations

Vermont Agency of Natural Resources, Department of Forests, Parks and Recreation (North Springfield office).

In the Area

The Scott Covered Bridge is often cited as the longest single-span covered bridge in Vermont. The original bridge, built in 1870 by Harrison Chamberlain, had one **town lattice** span 166 feet long—the longest single span in Vermont. Town lattice structure refers to diagonal crossing beams between king posts. As the West River eroded its banks, two additional **king post** bridges were added on the west end of the bridge, bringing its length to 276 feet. The Vermont Historic Sites Association hopes to fully restore the bridge, which is now closed to vehicular traffic.

Ledges Overlook Trail
Townshend Dam

- **1.7 miles, 400-foot elevation gain (and a short nature trail)**
- **2 hours**
- **difficult**
- **bring binoculars**

A vista of the West River Valley and a high perch from which to watch for wildlife and waterfowl, such as bald eagles, osprey, and loons.

The U.S. Army Corps of Engineers is greening up by making a concerted effort to manage its large landholdings around dam sites for environmental and recreational goals. At Townshend Dam, Corps personnel manage more than 1,000 acres of land to maintain a diversity of fish and wildlife habitats. Nest boxes attract breeding birds, including **wood ducks, mergansers, bluebirds,** and **tree swallows.** Rangers plant wildlife food plots and prune apple trees to increase the food supply for **deer, fox, ruffed grouse,** and **cedar waxwings.** Tracks and scat indicate the area is habitat for **whitetail deer, coyote, black bear, beaver, turkey, cottontail, raccoon, muskrat, otter, mink, porcupine, waterfowl,** and upland game birds. This trail provides a beautiful overview of the entire area and an opportunity to catch sight of birds, game, and waterfowl.

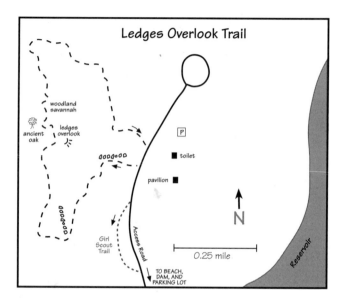

Ledges Overlook Trail

woodland savannah

ancient oak

ledges overlook

P

toilet

pavilion

N

Girl Scout Trail

Access Road

0.25 mile

Reservoir

TO BEACH, DAM, AND PARKING LOT

The trail begins on the left beyond the picnic pavilion. After several turns, we began climbing more steeply. At the top, the trail turns north and gradually ascends to the rock outcroppings, where we were more than happy to cast off our packs and sit for awhile. We were looking down upon the Townshend Reservoir and Dam. (Be very careful near the ledges, especially with children.) To the right lies the West River Valley. The river flows to Brattleboro, where it joins the Connecticut near the base of Wantastiquet Mountain (page 59). It has been a major route joining Lake Champlain with the Connecticut River for 8,000 years. Far to your right is the hump of Bald Mountain (page 81) and across the valley is Rattlesnake Mountain.

We saw several pairs of **loons** swimming on the reservoir, and a hawk circled overhead. Scan the trees along the water with your binoculars and watch for fishing **osprey.** You may see **bald eagles** as well. In the spring, many **waterfowl** stop here as they migrate. After enjoying the views, we continued across the ledge on the trail and soon came to an ancient red oak tree, three feet or more in diameter. The trail here is blazed (a little too conspicuously to my taste) in red and orange.

Shortly after the red oak, the trail leads through a small **woodland savannah,** composed of **hornbeam** trees with a grassy lawn beneath. This poor tree's name has spawned a huge amount of confusion—which I

A woodland savannah has a grassy forest floor with little or no understory.

won't pretend to unravel, but I can clarify the terms used here. The names **hornbeam, American hornbeam, hop hornbeam, Eastern hop hornbeam,** and **ironwood** are all used almost interchangeably for two different trees. The two trees involved are both of a very hard wood, but one has shreddy light-brown bark *(Ostrya virginiana)* and the other has smooth, muscular-looking gray bark *(Carpinus caroliniana)*. The confusion is not just in the use of popular names; it extends to professional disagreements among writers of tree identification guides. The same tree has to be looked up under different names in different guides. We will follow George A. Petrides in the *Peterson Field Guide to Trees* by calling the **shreddy-barked tree** "hornbeam" and the **smooth, muscular gray-barked tree** "ironwood." Old-timers kept them straight by calling the shreddy-barked tree "leverwood" and the smooth, muscular, gray-barked tree "musclewood," but unfortunately, these descriptive terms are no longer much in use.

Hornbeam is used to make tools that require a hard surface, such as wooden planes. Many people pass it by when cutting firewood because of how rapidly it will dull a chain, sometimes even throwing sparks off as you try to cut it. In any case, walking through an open stand of hornbeam in the grassy savannah is a quite different experience from walking in a hardwood forest. It offers a woodland sunny feeling that, as you come upon it, suddenly relieves the shadowed darkness of the forest.

The descending trail is rather rough and beginning to erode for lack of waterbars. As the slope of the trail becomes more gradual, **trout-lilies** (also known as

An unusually large hornbeam tree with characteristic shreddy bark. A photo of iron-wood, for comparison, appears on page 253.

adder's-tongue and, in Vermont, as **dog-tooth violets**) spread into the woods. Soon we were back on the access road north of where the trail began.

Girl Scout Nature Trail

The Girl Scout Nature Trail at the dam recreation area has a series of stations on it, each created by a Scout. My favorite, Station 11, suggests lying on your back and discovering pictures in the clouds while you feel the earth spinning a little. Station 12, along a small stream-cut ravine, asks:

Could you have stood where you are in April 1987? No, but a fish or two might have swam by. The dam was full. There would have been 100 feet of water over your head. The chance of the dam filling to 100% is once in 100 years, or once in a lifetime. Two pictures below were taken at the time of the flood.

The photos are gone, and some of the other stations are in poor repair. We hope that the Girl Scouts renew this wonderful little trail.

The West River and the 1987 Flood

The West River drains an area of 278 square miles, including runoff and snowmelt from three ski areas: Bromley, Magic Mountain, and Stratton. Local people remember the **flood of April 1987,** when the reservoir was 100 percent full (with a capacity of 11 billion gallons) and water cascaded over its spillway. The station on the Girl Scout Nature Trail provides a visceral sense of the enormous quantity of water held back by the dam at that time.

From the ledges, you can see the remains of old Route 30 running along the river. In pre-dam floods, the road was underwater and millions of dollars of damage was done to riverside homes, industries, and agricultural lands. Completed in 1961, the Townshend Dam, together with the Ball Mountain Dam farther upstream, control flooding on the river.

Though there has been some discussion about using the dam system to generate electricity, it presents a use conflict: a flood-control reservoir should be relatively empty so it can store floodwaters; conversely, a hydroelectric dam needs deep headwaters to drive its turbines.

Getting There

Townshend Dam is on Route 30 between Townshend and West Townshend. The dam is on your left going north on Route 30. Turn left at the dam and cross it. The first right leads into the Townshend Dam Recreation Area.

Affiliated Organizations

U.S. Army Corps of Engineers, Townshend Lake Office.

In the Area

On the Route 30 side of the dam is a pull-off and parking lot. This is an official vantage point for the **Watchable Wildlife Program** on Corps land. At the end of the parking lot, you can descend to the **West River Trail,** which goes north through river bottomland rich with birds, wildlife, and lots of active beavers.

Downstream of the dam, an **Atlantic salmon trap** is operated as part of the **anadromous fish** (those that migrate back upstream to the place of their birth in order to spawn) restoration project on the Connecticut River (see page 104).

Just down the road from the dam is Townshend State Park and Bald Mountain (page 81).

Hamilton Falls
Jamaica State Park

- **5-mile round-trip, 650 feet of ascent**
- **2.5–3 hours**
- **easy/moderate**

An easy stroll along the riverbank for several miles passes by giant glacial erratics. A short but steep up-and-down leads to Vermont's highest waterfalls — Hamilton Falls.

We left the parking area and followed the river. A short way up, the river slows and deepens in a pool called the Salmon Hole, where swimmers can enjoy a dip. We then came to the Dumplings—a group of huge **glacial erratics** in the river. Erratics are boulders carried by a glacier and dropped elsewhere when the ice melted. Climbing on them, I found **crescentic fractures** in their surface (see page 71). Shortly past them on the right, the park's **Overlook Trail** intersects the Railroad Bed Trail.

In about two miles, we came to a fork. The Railroad Bed Trail continues to the left along the river to Ball Mountain Dam. We cut off right on the **Hamilton Falls Trail,** which runs uphill along Cobb Brook. It was built to bring goods down to the railroad. We walked steadily uphill on it for about three-quarters of a mile, where we spotted a trail to the left. We descended on it steeply more than 300 feet back down to Cobb Brook. There we

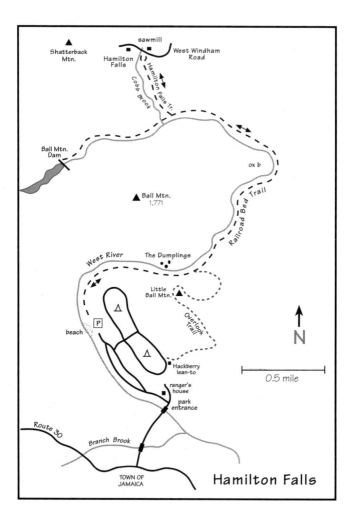

found ourselves at the base of the falls in a steep wood-land valley. The water cascades 125 feet downward through a series of chutes and pools carved into the granite. Because it is such a dramatic falls, there is a great temptation to cross the brook to climb up it or swim in one of its pools. **DON'T!** Eleven people have died trying to do just that.

To see the falls from the top, climb back up to the trail and continue up it a short distance until it ends at an unpaved road. Turn left, and just past the sawmill on your right, a short trail leads to the top of the falls. You

Hamilton Falls is Vermont's highest waterfall, cascading through several pools to the valley, 125 feet below.

return to the parking lot on the same trail that brought you here.

From Leaves in the Water to Trout on the Table

The West River provides good **trout fishing.** Here at the water's edge you can observe the steps in the **food chain** that lead to a nice fillet dinner. Begin by feeling a stone underwater. It is probably covered with slippery **algae**—at least on its downstream side. A minuscule layer of water against the stone is slowed by friction. This layer of slow-moving water is called the **boundary layer.** Many insects and their larvae—**stoneflies,**

Another world—the boundary layer—lies under the water on the downstream side of river rocks.

mayflies, and good old **blackflies** among them — depend on it to keep their eggs attached to rocks. You may see **blackfly larvae** swaying in the current when you lift a rock. They attach themselves firmly in place and filter food from the water with sievelike structures at their heads. Much of their food originates from leaves that fall into the river, adding fresh nutrients to the water.

Blackfly larvae can be so numerous they form a dark carpet over the rocks. If they become dislodged, they let out a silk strand like a spider and use it to pull themselves back upstream. Once stonefly and mayfly eggs hatch, their **nymphs** also remain in the boundary zone to graze algae and organic leaf matter. As they grow and transform, they become a rich source of food for trout. The trout, in turn, may end up on our table — making us feel very fortunate to be at the top of the food chain.

History of Jamaica State Park and the West River

As far back as 8,000 years, Native Americans traveled the West River in their canoes as a link in their route between Lake Champlain and the Connecticut River. Archaeologists believe that the site of today's Jamaica State Park was once a thriving Native American village or large campsite. When European settlers came up the West River, they began logging, farming, and harnessing the water to power their mills. Most of the Native Americans either left or died from diseases introduced by the settlers. The fortunes of the mills seemed to decline just as America was falling in love with the railroad. The West River Railroad went into service in 1881 between South Londonderry and Brattleboro. Known affectionately as **36 miles of trouble,** it never made money.

When the flood of 1927 washed away most of what was left of the railroad, the company finally called it quits. The tracks were torn up and sold for scrap, and the right-of-way passed to the state. A brochure available at the park describes the history of the railroad, replete with an old photo of one of the many train wrecks that resulted from the underfunded construction. Today, the old railroad bed is being transformed into the West River Trail for walkers, bicyclists, and crosscountry skiers.

The trail through Jamaica State Park follows the old railroad bed along the West River.

Getting There

Jamaica State Park is in the town of Jamaica on Route 30. A sign in Jamaica marks the turn to the north off Route 30 that leads to the park. The entrance to the park is on the left after crossing the second bridge.

Affiliated Organizations

Vermont Agency of Natural Resources, Department of Forests, Parks and Recreation (North Springfield office). Hamilton Falls is in a 41-acre tract designated as a State Natural Area.

In the Area

On a weekend in late April and another in late September, the U.S. Army Corps of Engineers releases water from the Ball Mountain and Townshend dams to create whitewater recreation days. When conditions permit, a truck ferry service at Jamaica State Park takes people and their water craft upstream to Cobb Brook. For a fee, other groups offer rafting trips on the river.

Several miles north on Route 30, a marked turn to the right leads into the Ball Mountain Dam and Recreation Area. Here the Railroad Bed Trail continues several miles north to the Winhall Brook Camping area. The dam at Ball Mountain is a Watchable Wildlife Area.

Petroglyphs and Fish Ladder

Bellows Falls

- **does not involve walking any distance**
- **1 hour**
- **very easy**
- **bring camera and binoculars**

*Although this location involves nature — the Connecticut
River, salmon, and rock carvings — it doesn't require
more than a few hundreds yards of walking.*

By visiting the petroglyphs first, you will get an overall
sense of the river and land that are responsible for the
fact that a power generating station and fish ladder are
located here. The Vilas Bridge on Bridge Street first
spans a canal and then the narrow, gorgelike bend in
the Connecticut River. Park in the municipal parking lot
immediately on the left after crossing the canal. From
the parking lot, cross the street and walk east toward
the bridge. Just before it, turn right on a dirt access
road. On the left is a guard rail whose posts are all blue
except for one — painted **orange.** It marks the vicinity
from which the petroglyphs can be seen. The carvings
are on the same side of the river that you are on. Some
paint splashes on the rocks below indicate their loca-

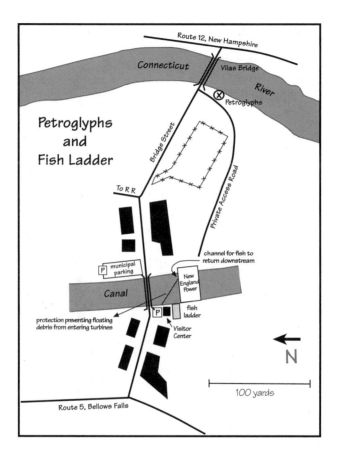

Petroglyphs and Fish Ladder

Route 12, New Hampshire

Connecticut

Vilas Bridge

River

⊗ Petroglyphs

Bridge Street

To R R

Private Access Road

channel for fish to return downstream

P municipal parking

New England Power

Canal

protection preventing floating debris from entering turbines

P

fish ladder

Visitor Center

N

100 yards

Route 5, Bellows Falls

tion. As you peer over, you will see primitive faces staring back up at you.

Although somewhat spoiled by the presence of today's bridge, it is apparent that this is a dramatic formation in the river. Native Americans called this river the **Quonehtokot,** from which the state of Connecticut and the river drew their names. It means "the long tidal river." This was the ideal spot for early peoples to catch salmon and shad as they migrated upstream through the narrows.

The petroglyphs are thought to have been discovered in the late eighteenth century or earlier. The carvings could date anywhere from several thousand to 400 years ago. Photographs and drawings made in the mid-nineteenth century show the images were of simple heads, with lines radiating from some of them. An 1857 drawing by an amateur archaeologist illustrated faces of varying sizes with simplistic eyes and mouths, many of them with horns or feathers.

One group of the Bellows Falls petroglyphs.

Early historians theorized that the carvings were simply idle drawings of the **Abenaki,** Native Americans who hunted and fished in Vermont. That notion, however has been largely discounted. Some genealogists, alluding to lines drawn between the faces, think the drawings illustrate familial relationships. Different experts have put forth many ideas of what they may commemorate: a celebration, a ritual ceremony, a skirmish with settlers, important tribal events — or a particularly successful catch of fish.

Fearing that the carvings were eroding, the local chapter of the Daughters of the American Revolution hired a stonecutter in the 1930s (horrors!) to deepen many of the original carvings so they would be more distinct. Then, in 1961 — with the best of intentions and the worst of results — the local Chamber of Commerce had the carvings outlined in yellow paint so people could see them better. The pictograms themselves remain an intriguing legacy of those who inhabited this land before us.

Fish Ladder, Powerhouse, and Visitor Center

The fish ladder is located at the New England Power Company Visitor Center, just west of the municipal parking lot on the other side of the street. By seeing the gorge and the petroglyphs before visiting the fish ladder, you'll appreciate how the river has cut deeply through the rocks on a sharp bend. This geologic feature precipitated a number of historical events.

The Connecticut River — at 407 miles long, New England's longest — was the first major river in the United States to be improved for travel; almost 250 miles were opened for navigation by 1810. However, after visiting the petroglyphs, you can see that this narrows and the highest waterfall on the Connecticut—at more than 60 feet—presented a formidable obstacle to transportation. In 1792, work began on a timber dam to divert the river's waters into the **first navigational canal** in the United States, built with a series of nine locks. Local history recounts how a side-wheeler boat that was too large to fit in the canal was once hauled up the streets of Bellows Falls.

By the mid-1880s, railroads had largely replaced the river as a means of transportation, so the canal's waters were diverted into sluiceways to power local mills. By 1898, a utility was **generating electricity** using the canal's waters. In 1928, the New England Power Company took over the site and built the present concrete dam and Georgian Revival–style powerhouse on the site where the former canal veered sharply to the southwest.

Before the first dams were built on the Connecticut River in the 1700s, **Atlantic salmon** swam upstream to spawn in its tributaries. The Connecticut had one of the largest runs of Atlantic salmon in North America, with the salmon ascending the river as far as 372 miles north to Beecher Falls. When impassable dams were built, the salmon could no longer reach their natural spawning ground and consequently, after 1800, there were few salmon to be found in the river.

The **American shad,** which spawned in the river's main channel, could migrate only about the first 80 miles of the river in Connecticut. Congress sought to remedy the situation by passing the **Great Lakes and**

Anadromous Fisheries Restoration Act of 1965, which, for the first time, provided federal cost-sharing for programs that would restore the unobstructed migration of these fish. New Hampshire, Vermont, Massachusetts, and Connecticut, in cooperation with the **U.S. Fish and Wildlife Service** and the **National Marine Fisheries Service,** took advantage of the federal program to restore Atlantic salmon and American shad to the Connecticut River and its tributaries.

Construction of the fish ladder at the **New England Power plant** in Bellows Falls began in May 1982 and began operation in 1984. Salmon were reintroduced to

The New England Power fish ladder at Bellows Falls.

the upper Connecticut for the first time since the 1790s, when the river was dammed for the canal. The **fish ladder** enables Atlantic salmon, American shad, and other fish to pass from the dam's tailrace, located below the station, to the canal above the station, where they continue their journey north to tributaries in the upper river. The fish move up the ladder in much the same way earlier canal boats moved up the locks. The ladder itself consists of 66 pools, each a foot higher than the previous pool. Water cascades from one to the next, emulating river rapids and providing an upstream route for the migrating fish.

A working model of the station and fish ladder are located in the Visitor Center, with headphones for learning about the functioning of the fish ladder and the powerhouse. Downstairs, a glass wall provides an underwater view into the ladder. If you are there between April and early July and you are lucky, you might see a shad or salmon negotiating the ladder against the current. A video of the operation is shown at the center, as well as displays relating to fish, the river, and other recreational areas owned and managed by New England Power.

The Atlantic Salmon

The Atlantic salmon is an **anadromous** fish, which means *running upstream.* It spawns in freshwater, migrate to salt water to feed and mature, and then, completing its cycle, returns to freshwater to spawn. Unlike Pacific salmon, which die after spawning, the Atlantic species may breed for several years. The Atlantic salmon spends its first year near its birthplace in fresh-water, growing four to six inches long, when it becomes known as a **parr.** It usually takes a parr up to two years to grow to seven or eight inches or more—the size it needs to begin its journey downstream to the ocean.

When it reaches the ocean, it smolts, adapting to saltwater life, and is then known as a **smolt.** The smolt spends at least two summers and two winters traveling long distance in salt water, while feeding on crustaceans and growing to a weight of about 15 pounds. When it reaches breeding age as a **salmon,** it is ready to return to its birthplace the next spring to spawn. When it is ready to swim upstream in freshwater, it changes its diet to small fish.

It reaches its spawning grounds by late October or early November. There it occupies a gravelly area in a river tributary, and the female releases an average of 7,500 eggs, which are fertilized and deposited in gravel nests, called **redds.** They remain there over the winter and, in the spring, hatch as **alevin.** Initially, the alevin remain in the gravel substrate, absorbing their yolk sacs. Between mid-May and early June, at an inch and a quarter long, the tiny **fry** emerge from the redd, ready to start feeding in the stream.

Of the original 7,500 eggs spawned, about 4,500 will hatch successfully into fry. Predators such as **trout, herons,** and **kingfishers** reduce their numbers to 250 by the end of their first summer. Overwinter losses leave about 100 by the following year. Only about 50 survive two years and grow to seven or eight inches, but these are now ready for their journey to the sea.

From tagging smolts in hatcheries and monitoring them after release, the **Connecticut River Atlantic Salmon Commission** has developed a picture of their lives at sea. During May and June, the smolts enter the ocean. By early July, they are off the coast of Nova Scotia. In August, the salmon, now about 15 inches or more in length, have migrated to the southern coast of Newfoundland. In another year, salmon from all eastern rivers are in waters where they are exposed to being caught by **commercial fishermen** from **Canada** and western **Greenland.** It is estimated that commercial fishing reduces the salmon population at sea by another 50 percent or more. On their return, they migrate upriver between April and early July, though most of them can be seen passing up the fish ladders from mid-May to mid-June.

The Commission's goal is to ensure that the numbers of salmon returning to the river continues to increase in the years ahead, leading to a significant wild spawning population. The restocking efforts include both federal and state fish culture facilities, which together hold up to 1,000 adult salmon and incubate 3.5 million eggs, 2 million fry, and 500,000 smolts annually. As of 1994, a total of 3,731 Atlantic salmon had returned to the Connecticut, and it is now possible to use their progeny in the restoration program. Because of fish ladders, salmon can return as far north as the Ammonoosuc River in New Hampshire for the first time in more than 175 years.

Getting There

Both the fish ladder and petroglyphs are located on Bridge Street in Bellows Falls. From US 5, in the center of Bellows Falls, take Bridge Street (Route 12 west) toward New Hampshire. Drive over the canal and immediately on your left is the municipal parking lot.

The Visitor Center at the power station is open May to October, but the fish ladder itself only operates when the fish are spawning. That occurs sometime between April and early July. At this writing, the Visitor Center is closed Tuesdays and Wednesdays. For information on the schedule and salmon run, call New England Power at 802-463-3226.

Affiliated Organizations

Petroglyphs: Greater Falls Regional Chamber of Commerce.

Fish Ladder: New England Power Company. There is handicapped parking at the Visitor Center and access to and through the building to view the fish ladder.

Manchester Area

Prospect Rock
Green Mountain National Forest, Manchester Depot

- **3-mile round-trip, 1,000-foot elevation gain**
- **2–3 hours**
- **difficult**
- **bring a camera, binoculars, good walking shoes**

An uphill walk leads to a great view of Mt. Equinox and the Valley of Vermont. Its mixed forests make it a spectacular trail in the fall.

This is one of the very few real hikes in this guide, but it is not overly ambitious, and the view from Prospect Rock itself is a great reward for the effort. From the trailhead, the old jeep road you will follow makes an almost perfect beeline to Prospect Rock. Most of the elevation is gained in the first mile, and then the trail levels out. We began in a mixed hardwood/hemlock forest and walked up a shallow valley that follows a stream on the right. Brooks cascade from the mountain-

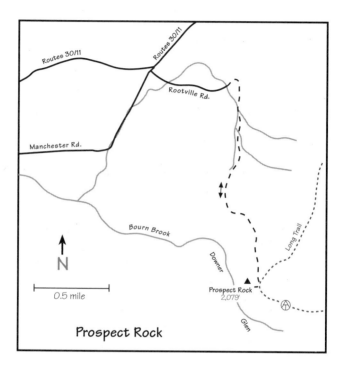

Prospect Rock

side to join the stream, and the trail crosses several of them, one on a wooden bridge.

About three-quarters of a mile up, we left the brook behind. **Common elderberry** was growing on the right, something that always reminds me of my grandfather's homemade elderberry wine, which he made each fall. He always offered it—and the family always accepted—but I never saw him take even a sip. Then to the west, glimpses of Downer Glen appear through

through the trees. There are some very old yellow and paper birch in this area, while many other of the hardwood trees are disappearing as the elevation increases.

The slope to the right is steep, and we were actually looking into the tops of trees growing from below. The road continues to level out to a very gradual incline, and at about 2,000 feet in elevation, we began to see **spruce** and **fir trees.** They are mixed with many other deciduous trees at this elevation, but if you were to climb higher mountains, you would see that by 3,000 feet, the forest would have changed to that of the **northern boreal forest,** composed primarily of spruce and fir (see page 199).

We spotted the **double white blaze** on the left that marks the **Appalachian Trail/Long Trail** where it intersects the road. Right across from this intersection are

The Sunday AM Amblers pose here atop the billion-year old Prospect Rock.

several short trails that lead out, in 50 yards or so, to **Prospect Rock.** It is perched spectacularly above Downer Glen, with mighty **Mt. Equinox** (elev. 3,816 feet) directly across the valley to the west. The elevation of Prospect Rock is 2,079 feet. As we sat down on Prospect Rock, a **yellow-bellied sapsucker** flew by just below us.

As we looked out over the edge, directly below us was a vast hillside of solid white birch. It appeared as though the trees were growing horizontally out of the side of the ledge. Manchester is below, in the **Valley of Vermont,** which stretches almost due north-south from the Massachusetts border up to Lake Bomoseen, where it joins the Champlain Valley Lowland.

We returned the way we came—only in about one-third of the time.

The Valley of Vermont (A Billion Years in a Nutshell)

The ridge of mountains you see from Prospect Rock, including Mt. Equinox, is part of the Taconic Range, which lies across the Valley of Vermont from the Green Mountains. The valley is a feature you are well aware of if you've ever driven US 7 in southern Vermont. How the mountain ranges and the valley between them came to be is an interesting and unusual story.

The earth's crust started to form at least 4.5 billion years ago. More than a billion years ago, sediments built up at the bottom of the **continental shelf** of a much smaller North American continent. Then, in the middle of the ocean, the earth's crust caved inward, drawing the continents together. As they collided (very slowly in geologic time), the rock that had formed from the sediments on the continental shelf was thrust upward and compressed, buckled, and deformed under unimaginable forces of heat and pressure.

This activity formed a ridge of north-south mountains called the **ancient Adirondacks.** Over hundreds of millions of years, this mountain range eroded away until it was covered by a shallow sea. The bedrock at the bottom of the range remained, however, and in due time became the core of the Green Mountains. Today, from Rutland to the Massachusetts border, this **Precambrian rock** (meaning it was formed before multicellular life-forms appeared) is exposed on some of the summits in the Green Mountains, such as Killington and Pico. As you sit on Prospect Rock itself, you can contemplate the incredible fact that it was formed about *one billion years ago*. The Precambrian rock in the Green Mountains is the **oldest rock in New England**...but we're getting ahead of ourselves.

About 650 million years ago (after the ancient Adirondacks had worn down but long before the Green Mountains were formed), the continents began drifting apart again and formed a new ocean between them. It wasn't the Atlantic Ocean we know today; it was an earlier Atlantic, called the **proto-Atlantic Ocean.** As the continents drifted apart, they stretched the earth's crust. The plains formed of the bedrock of the ancient Adirondacks ended up as a new continental shelf, flooded by a shallow sea. The area then underwater included most of what is today New York State and western New England.

In the **Cambrian period** — a little more than 500 million years ago — there was an explosion of new life-forms, including many shelled creatures in the oceans. The shells of these ancient organisms and coral began piling up on the continental shelf. Over millions of years, this layer became several miles thick and, through compression, became limestone. (A similar activity was happening offshore in deeper waters, where shale, sandstone, and mudstone were forming.) As you look into and northward up the Valley of Vermont from Prospect Rock, the limestone floor of that ancient continental shelf, much eroded and deformed, is what you see, but it is no longer underwater, and you are sitting 1,000 feet above it. How did that happen?

Easy. The continents, once separated by the proto-Atlantic Ocean, began drifting back together again. In fact, all of the earth's continents drifted slowly back together to form one huge supercontinent geologists call **Pangea,** which existed until about 200 to 250 million years ago. Today's **ferns** and **spikemosses** (page 162) are related to the tree-sized plants that were growing on land as Pangea formed. As fern-trees grew, died, and decayed for millions of years, they eventually formed today's coal deposits.

In the process of Pangea's forming, Europe and Africa drifted back toward North America. Their movement, plus volcanic activity, pushed up a chain of islands between them. This chain of islands—called the **Bronson Hill Island Arc**—was eventually squeezed against the coast of North America, where it—and parts of Europe and Africa—remained when the continents separated the last time. Wantastiquet Mountain (page 59) was originally part of this island chain, and Boston and much of New England's coast were a piece of

From Prospect Rock in the Green Mountains, the Valley of Vermont can be seen stretching north, with the Taconic Mountains forming its western side.

Europe and Africa left behind.

As Pangea formed by the converging continents, parts of the coast of what was then North America were uplifted in two mountain-building events: the **Taconic orogeny,** which began about 460 million years ago (and in which the Bronson Hill Island Arc was formed) and the **Acadian orogeny,** about 400 million years ago.

The pressure on our coast (located then about where eastern Vermont is today) was massive, and there was much crumpling and thrusting and folding of the layers of rock that formed the edge of North America, and these effects stretched far inland. As you drive Vermont's major highways and interstates, you can see the complex results of these events in the misshapen, fractured, and angular thrusting in the layers of rock exposed by road cuts. The folding and faulting that occurred thrust up the pre-Cambrian ancient Adirondack bedrock. Forced upward, the pre-Cambrian rock and the miles-thick layer of rock covering it rose up to become the Green Mountains. In the midst of the heat and pressure of these events, much of the existing rock and sediment throughout Vermont metamorphosed — e.g. **limestone** in the Valley of Vermont was turned into **marble** and **shale** became **slate** (see page 178).

That's how the mountain you are sitting on came to be, but that's not how Mt. Equinox and the Taconics across the valley came to be. In fact, where the Taconics came from is a world-famous mystery. Their formation took place at about the same time as the Green Mountains, but they couldn't have formed the same way.

The problem geologists are wrestling with — and they haven't all come to an agreement — is this: the rock that forms the Taconics is actually **older than the bedrock upon which it sits.** They simply could not have been formed where they sit today. They had to have been transported there from somewhere else!

One explanation is that the Taconic Range is formed of rock that originated as deep sea sediments that were thrust westward, sliding up and over first the continental shelf and then the continental plate itself. This landmass eventually slid down the western side of the Green Mountains — which were being formed at the time. Since then, erosion formed the valley between the two mountain ranges.

Other geologists, noticing that the summits of the southern Green Mountains are the oldest rock in all of

New England, wonder what happened to the layer of younger rock that must have covered these peaks, just as it does in the Green Mountains of northern Vermont. They speculate that the top of the Green Mountains was pushed off and settled across the valley as the Taconics. Still others hypothesize that sedimentary layers flipped upside down as the mountains were forming. These theories provide an overly simple glimpse into the kinds of issues that excite geologists.

When a land mass is pushed or otherwise moved onto younger rocks, it is called a **klippe.** Sitting on Prospect Rock and looking across the valley at massive Mt. Equinox, you are looking at the eastern edge of the **Taconic Klippe,** which extends westward as far as the Hudson River. Its eastern edge is actually a series of stacked thrust faults, which might be likened to what happens to a deck of cards when you drop them on the floor.

Once the Taconics and the Green Mountains formed, the Valley of Vermont remained between them—a valley whose limestone bedrock makes it a region of rich soils. There is also talc, slate, and marble that formed from the limestone and shale. A talc mine in the Taconics is visible from US 7 in South Wallingford. As you drive north on US 7, you cannot help but notice the valley walls rising on either side and growing closer together. Near North Dorset, where US 7 passes Emerald Lake (page 142), the valley is at its narrowest—only several hundred yards separate the two mountain ranges, barely wide enough to accommodate US 7, a railroad track, and the lake itself.

Getting There

Prospect Rock is just east of Manchester Center. Coming from the east on Routes 30/11, the Manchester Ranger Station for the Green Mountain National Forest is on the left. Go 0.4 mile farther and turn left at the sign for East Manchester Road. Immediately on your left as you make the turn is another left turn, onto unpaved Rootville Road. (Coming from Manchester, this intersection is 0.5 mile beyond the junction of US 7 with Routes 30/11.) Once on Rootville Road, go about 0.5 mile to its end. Turn around and park on the right-hand side of the road, being careful not to block the driveway and respecting the "No Parking" signs in the turn-around area. The trail is the continuation of Rootville Road as it leads into the forest.

Affiliated Organizations

Green Mountain National Forest, Green Mountain Club, and Appalachian Trail Conference.

In the Area

From Prospect Rock, you are overlooking the Manchester area, which offers two other nearby nature walks: the Pond Loop Trail (next page) on Mt. Equinox and the Boswell Botany Trail (page 129).

If you are interested in learning more about marble, visit the Vermont Marble Exhibit, the world's largest marble museum, located on Main Street in Proctor. (Proctor is 40 miles north of Manchester on US 7.) For more information, call 802-459-2300.

Pond Loop Trail
Equinox Preservation Trust, Manchester

- **2.25 miles (0.75 mile, 300-foot elevation gain to Robin's Lookout)**
- **1.5–2 hours (45-minute round-trip to Robin's Lookout)**
- **easy (moderate to Robin's Lookout)**

A walk through a rich northern hardwood forest to beautiful Equinox Pond and a short climb to an overlook of the pond, the Battenkill Valley, and the Green Mountains.

The Equinox Preservation Trust protects 850 acres from the valley to near the ridgeline of Mt. Equinox (elev. 3,816 feet)—the highest peak in the Taconic Range. The Trust, formed in 1993 by Equinox Resort Associates, is a partnership whose members include the Vermont Land Trust, the Vermont Institute of Natural Science (VINS), The Nature Conservancy, Bennington College, and the Burr and Burton Seminary.

There is an extensive trail system, but since the slopes are steep, most of them involve uphill hiking. We selected an easy trail through Equinox's hardwood forest and a stroll around serene **Equinox Pond.** With a short, modest climb, **Robin's Lookout** provides a great view. To obtain a copy of the excellent and informative map/brochure for

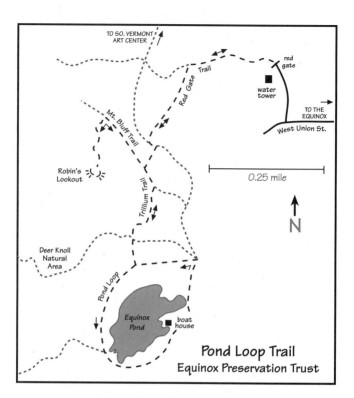

Pond Loop Trail
Equinox Preservation Trust

the entire trust trail system, and to obtain advice on parking, stop first at the desk of The Equinox, an elegant hotel
on Route 7A in Manchester Village.

We walked up Red Gate Trail on an old logging
road, and shortly came to a patch of **coltsfoot.** This is a
strange early spring plant that goes through its complete flowering cycle before it bears leaves. Its yellow

flowers are similar to a dandelion's, but have many more fine petals. Its stem has reddish scales and looks something like Indian pipes. The flower goes to seed in a sphere, again like a dandelion. Only then do its very large leaves start to grow.

In about 10 minutes, we came to where the Red Gate and Blue trails diverge. We turned left to remain on the Red Gate Trail. We passed through a small clearing and came to a trail junction. We went left on the Trillium Trail, which cuts to the right 50 yards farther. A **rose-breasted grosbeak** was sitting on a branch at the trail's side, singing and watching us go by. Roger Tory Peterson aptly describes its mellow song by saying it sounds as if it were a robin who took voice lessons. It sings throughout the day, when many other songbirds are quiet.

Equinox Pond at the foot of Mt. Equinox.

We are in a **rich northern hardwood forest,** full of healthy trees and abundant ground cover. This is exceptionally fertile soil, because the bedrock is high in calcium and nutrients, and new nutrients constantly wash down the steep slopes. Nowhere else in Vermont do these conditions exist so extensively as on this face of Equinox. Such forests are equally uncommon in the adjoining states of New Hampshire and New York.

This land was cleared in the past, but these younger trees, now protected, will grow into an old-growth forest in a century or so. Evidence of earlier logging can be seen clearly along portions of the trail. Wounds at the base of many of the trees still exist where the bark was scraped off.

As we neared the Pond Loop Trail on the Trillium Trail, we entered a forest of **eastern white pine,** and the trail became soft with their needles. **Equinox Pond** nestles among the trees on the mountain's lower flank. We strolled quietly and slowly around it, enjoying the solitude and watching the reflections of the mountain shimmer in its blue-green waters. The beauty of this small, perfect pond hushes conversation. A man floated lazily on its waters in a small boat, his fishing line in the water. The trail crossed the inlet stream on a small bridge and led us to the boat house, built in the style of an Adirondack camp. The rose-breasted grosbeak's song again and a **rufous-sided towhee** (a wavering *drink-your-teeeee*) were the only sounds to break the afternoon's silence.

We started to return by again taking the Trillium Trail. You can return to the Red Gate, or take the Mt.

Bluff Trail to Robin's Lookout. All trails are clearly marked at their intersection, and if you've stopped for a map at The Equinox, you'll see that you have many other options as well. We ascended the Mt. Bluff Trail a short distance and cut-off left to climb to Robin's Lookout. The sheer profusion of plant varieties on the forest floor is amazing—a product of the rich soils. In one square-foot section, I counted 16 different plants, ferns, and mosses. In the spring, **violets, spring-beauties,** and **jack-in-the-pulpits** lined the trail. Many rare and unusual plants grow on the mountainside. They include **Goldie's fern,** the giant of the woodferns; **wild millet,** which is a cornfield weed in heartland states but rare here; and **squawroot,** a parasitic plant found growing from tree roots, usually oaks. It is in the broomrape family and grows a stubby, scaled, fleshy stalk with a spike of hooded yellow flowers.

We climbed steeply for a short distance and then walked over a series of mossy knolls. Checking tree cavities and the high spots where squirrels love to eat, I found shells from both **butternut** and **pignut hickory,** though I didn't see the trees in the immediate vicinity.

At last we came to the lookout, 300 feet above Equinox Pond. It provides a breathtaking view of the pond, the Battenkill Valley, and the Green Mountains. To the northeast, you can see Downer Glen, though Prospect Rock (page 111) itself is not visible. For a 15- to 20-minute walk up, this is a great view. Once you've rested and enjoyed this spot, retrace your steps back to the Red Gate.

At the Pond's Surface

Standing at the edge of Equinox Pond, we saw the sun and trees reflecting off of it, but the water's surface is more than a mirror: it is a microhabitat zone for many kinds of life. Scientists call this zone of surface tension the **neuston.**

When **water striders** skate on the water's surface, they make good use of their four pairs of legs: the hind-most pair are the runners; the next pair are the drivers; the third pair are used to steer; and the front pair are held at the ready to capture food. Clever engineer that nature is—its tiny grasping claws are set back on its legs to ensure that the strider doesn't accidentally break the surface tension.

A water strider casts his characteristic shadow while waiting for a meal to be washed downstream.

The molecular bonds that create the phenomenon of surface tension may not be a strong force, but to the tiny critters that live there, it is as essential as gravity is to us. If you were to catch a strider and put it in a jar of water, it would probably drown as the water sloshes and the surface tension is broken. In fact, microscopic creatures that live underwater can accidentally break through the surface of the water and be stranded on top of it to die.

Mosquito larvae, called **wrigglers,** are about a quarter-inch long. They have a breathing tube so they can stay on the underside of the water's surface but breathe through their "snorkel." The female lays her raft of eggs on the surface tension. If she's had a blood meal at your cost, her egg mass is larger and more eggs hatch.

Of the 30,000 kinds of beetles in the United States, only one type inhabits the neuston: crazy-to-watch **whirligigs.** They appear in large groups and remind me of bumper cars at an amusement park. Their tiny legs beat 60 times a second as they whip about, looking for food. They have two sets of eyes: one pair for looking across the top of the water and another pair for looking below it. Among their neighbors are many more animals that live or feed in this sliver of a habitat. Some are visible, like fish spiders and water treaders, and many others are seen only with a microscope.

Like Lewis Carroll's *Through the Looking Glass,* you enter a second world when you pass through the water's surface tension. On its underside are found snails and many other kinds of creatures feeding or hanging down. With a little patience and a magnifying glass, there is much more to be observed at the water's surface than the reflections of trees.

Getting There

The Equinox is located at the southern end of Manchester Village on Historic Route 7A. Check first at the hotel desk for a map and parking instructions.

Affiliated Organizations

Equinox Preservation Trust.

In the Area

Among potential destinations at Equinox are Deer Knoll, Table Rock, and Cook's Hollow. All have been known to botanists since 1899 for their unique assemblage of plants. Their use is restricted to enable the return of vegetation—including some rare species—that were damaged by past users. Please respect all trail sign requests.

A hiking trail leads from the trust lands to the Southern Vermont Art Center (page 134). A mile or more in length, depending on your starting point, it is easy walking except for a challenging downhill to the art center itself at the end.

Boswell Botany Trail
Southern Vermont Art Center, Manchester

- **0.75 mile, 45–60 minutes**
- **very easy**
- **bring a camera and wildflower guide book**

This woodland trail through a beautiful botanical garden offers identification of many native trees and wildflowers and representatives of most of Vermont's known ferns.

In 1964, this nature trail was created by Mrs. Harold H. "Petie" Boswell. In 1983, the Manchester Garden Club and the Trustees of Southern Vermont Artists, Inc., named this beautiful and educational walk the **Boswell Botany Trail.** With the approval of the Southern Vermont Art Center, the Garden Club of Manchester maintains the trails and plantings.

The Botany Trail is a leisurely woodland trail of ferns, trees, and wildflowers, many with a permanent identification marker. Old paper birch and other trees provide the canopy that creates such a hospitable woodland plant environment and add to its beauty. The setting artfully combines the formality of a garden with the feel of a natural setting. It is not a garden of exotics and ornamentals. To the contrary, the plant selection is

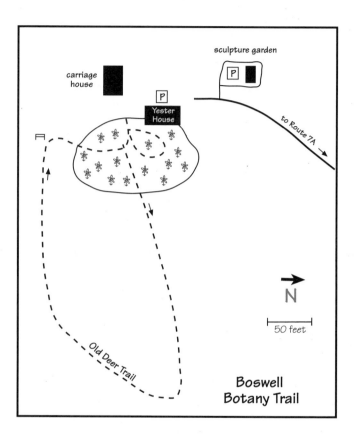

carriage
house

sculpture garden

P

Yester
House

to Route 7A →

N

50 feet

Old Deer Trail

Boswell
Botany Trail

one that reflects those **native species and varieties** seen throughout Vermont.

Of the 47 ferns that grow in Vermont, the Botany Trail leads you past 36 of them—and the Garden Club plants new flora each year. Some of the paper birches have died and were simply cut up in place and left to return to the soil. I am amazed at the work that must have been done to prepare the soil and create this garden in the midst of forested terrain—roots, rocks, and all.

This is a place where you wander more than walk. The Old Deer Trail leads downhill, beyond the formal plantings, and then loops back uphill to a lovely high point with rustic benches.

Open grasslands surround Yester House, home of the art center. They provide a beautiful setting for its collection of outdoor sculpture. A 285-year-old sugar maple at the edge of the woods behind the house adds a sense of timelessness to the modern art. Plan to spend some time in this elegant atmosphere exploring the gallery and grounds.

Sculpture appears throughout the grounds of the Southern Vermont Art Center and Boswell Botany Trail.

George D. Aiken on Wildflowers

George D. Aiken, a resident of Putney, Vermont, was first a Vermont governor who was then elected to the U.S. Senate in 1941. There he served for many years, becoming known as the Dean of the Senate for his unassuming wisdom and thoughtful approach to issues (Aiken, however, always preferred being called governor). He became well known for his proposal to simply declare ourselves the winners and get out of Vietnam 10 years before we did just that.

Governor Aiken was among the first to notice the disappearance of wildflowers from the wild as a result of avid picking. His labor of love for many years was developing ways to grow and reproduce wildflowers in a nursery, so that people would no longer have to uproot them from their natural settings. The Putney Nursery, established by Aiken, still operates in Putney, Vermont. When Governor Aiken was asked at age 84 if he still chased around the woods looking for wildflowers, he serenely replied: "No. They come to me now."

The introduction to his classic work, *Pioneering with Wildflowers,* originally published in 1935, has led to the education and conservation efforts of people like Petie Boswell and the many volunteers through the years who have maintained the Boswell Botany Trail and its plantings.

With thanks to the publisher, here is an excerpt of Governor Aiken's call to save wildflowers:

> In the Showy Ladyslipper, I see the Jesuits of France, their canoes breasting the currents of mighty rivers, as they plunge deeper and deeper

Bunchberry in bloom.

into the forests to establish the outposts of civilization in the far flung recesses of the vast Canadian wilderness.

The Poppy Mallow, sprawling with brilliant splashes of color on the baked Western plains, presents long lines of covered wagons, creeping scarcely faster than the Mallow itself, as home-seekers risk all to follow the sunset to their promised land.

And the Hepaticas, Bloodroots, Violets and Columbine, in them is colonial New England— school days, homemade clothes and bare feet, the bunch of flowers shyly placed on the teacher's desk, childhood games, laughter and sorrow.

Yes, the wildflowers have seen the development of the comforts of our so-called civilization.

They have seen the forests cut away, cities and villages grow up, roads made, bogs and marshes drained for agricultural purposes, great reservoirs built, flooding the fertile basins, and with each new development they have suffered....

We must learn how to propagate and grow all worthwhile species, and the purpose of this book is to give others, in plain, non-technical language some of the knowledge of wildflower requirements which I have learned during the last ten years.

The old frontier days of America are over, but the last stand of some of our wildflowers presents to us a new frontier in which we can adventure and that is why I call this book, "Pioneering with Wildflowers."

—George D. Aiken, 1935

Aiken's recently reprinted *Pioneering with Wildflowers* may be obtained directly from the publisher: Alan C. Hood & Company, 28 Birge Street, Brattleboro, VT 05301; 802-254-2200. The $14.95 price includes postage.

Getting There

The Southern Vermont Art Center is located on West Road in Manchester Village. West Road forks off Historic Route 7A to the west at the Mark Skinner Library. Go 0.7 mile and turn left at the entrance to the art center. The entrance gate is locked at 5:00 P.M.

*Maidenhair ferns
thrive at Boswell.*

Affiliated Organizations

Southern Vermont Art Center. No fee for walking; fee for entry to the art center's exhibits and gallery.

In the Area

The Pond Loop Trail (page 121) at the Equinox Preservation Trust is only a short distance away. A mile-long trail that is steep in parts connects them.

Merck Forest & Farmland Center

Rupert

- **Discovery Trail 0.75 mile (45 minutes); Tree Identification Trail 0.25 mile (15 minutes)**
- **allow extra time to enjoy the working farm**
- **very easy/easy**

A working farm, two nature trails, and wonderful views are all within an easy walk at this 2,800-acre forest and farm educational area.

The drive into the Merck Visitor Center passes through beautiful tree plantations—the products of George Merck's vision of conserving natural resources. Merck, former president of Merck Pharmaceuticals (then a family-owned business), personally established the Forest and Farmland Center as a nonprofit organization before his death in 1957 (Merck Pharmaceuticals does not fund the organization). Two trails and an old town road connect the center with the working farm. We walked the Discovery Trail to the farm, spent some time enjoying the views and animals, and returned via the Tree Identification Trail.

Discovery Trail

As we started on the Discovery Trail from the parking area, we immediately noticed that trees had been clear-

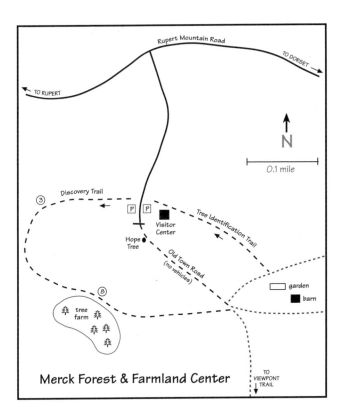

Merck Forest & Farmland Center

cut. A stand of **aspen** was being managed to develop **ruffed grouse habitat** (see below). The path follows an old road downhill. Just in the woods behind the sign for Stop 3 is a huge spreading **white ash** that is a **dominant tree** — one that has succeeded in spreading its crown over its rivals.

The two-acre aspen clear-cut can be seen at Stop 8. To the right, beyond the stone fence, is the Christmas tree farm. There are six- to eight-foot high **spruce trees,** but beyond them, rows of **balsam fir** are planted. We wandered down beyond the spruce and saw that the fir trees were less than a foot high and misshapen from frequent deer browse, strong evidence that—given a choice—deer prefer fir.

The trail then ascends to the farm. It is a working farm, not a petting zoo, and a variety of farm animals—including two Belgian draft horses—are about. However, a visitor recently thought he saw a draft horse crossing the field, but it turned out to be a moose. The farm's setting, with sweeping views and broad beautiful hillside meadows and pasture, is reminiscent of the inspiring set of *The Sound of Music.*

You can return the short distance back to the Visitor Center on Old Town Road, where the interior of a majestic oak has rotted out, making a cavity 12 to 15 feet high—large enough to walk in. Director Richard Thompson-Tucker said it is called the **Hope Tree,** because every year that the leaves come back out, there's still hope. We opted, however, to return on the Tree Identification Trail.

Tree Identification Trail

The Tree Identification Trail is parallel with Old Town Road and begins just above the fenced-in garden. The brochure for the walk identifies a dozen trees. We found 13 (adding a **gray birch**—whose leaf is distinctive from the other birches by its long narrow tip). The trail

A look inside the Hope Tree.

passes through stands of **European larch** and **eastern larch** (**tamarack**) that George Merck planted in 1951 to convert open land to valuable trees. He planted these two species to see if deer had a preference. Evidently they preferred neither, at least during the summer months when many more delectable buds and twigs are available. During winter, when hungry deer are all about, the larches drop their needles.

Soon you are back at the Visitor Center, where a new small shop has opened and you can obtain information about camping and the many educational programs run at the center.

Aspen (Popple)

Quaking and **bigtooth aspen,** along with other poplars, are often referred to simply as **popple** by Vermonters. Cottony aspen seeds carry far, making it one of the most widespread trees in the U.S. However, aspen also reproduces by sending up sucker shoots from its roots, creating genetically identical stands. The aspen at Merck were too mature and tall to serve as habitat and food for **ruffed grouse** and **woodcock,** which feed on aspen buds in the winter. These fowl also make use of popple cover for courtship and protection from predators.

By clear-cutting the mature aspen and clearing the surrounding area, the root systems are stimulated to send up new sprouts. Aspen grows rapidly, putting on as much as six feet of new growth in a season, and, because it propagates vegetatively, it can replenish itself

From high in the field, the Merck barnyard can be seen.

even if heavily browsed. **Whitetail deer** browse it, and **snowshoe hare** and **moose** feed on its bark and twigs year-round. If the mature aspen were not clear-cut here, they would eventually die off and be replaced by a northern hardwood forest, destroying favored habitat for grouse and the other animals who make use of it.

Getting There

Merck sits close to the New York State border in Rupert, east of Dorset. From the center of Dorset on Route 30, go north 1.9 miles and turn left onto Town Highway 315, Rupert Mountain Road. At 2.6 miles, the road crests the hill. Turn left at the sign to Merck.

Affiliated Organizations

The Merck Forest & Farmland Center is a community-supported nonprofit organization.

In the Area

Merck Forest offers nearly 28 miles of trails. Several are especially recommended. The hike to Mt. Antone is five miles round-trip, with about an 800-foot elevation gain to summit views that include the northern Catskills, the southern Adirondacks, and the White Creek Valley. The trail to Spruce Peak is about a three-mile round-trip from the parking lot and climbs 630 feet to beautiful views of the Merck area. Other trails lead to secluded overnight shelters. The Merck staff is happy to recommend a hike that meets your ability and schedule.

Emerald Lake Nature Trail
Emerald Lake State Park

- **0.75 mile, small hill**
- **45 minutes**
- **easy**

Emerald Lake Nature Trail is a short, easy walk with historical and natural points of interest. It is an excellent trail to see the profusion of plant varieties that thrive in the alkaline soils of the Valley of Vermont.

Emerald Lake State Park is located in a neck of land where the Taconic and the Green Mountain ranges come to within a few hundred yards of one another. It marks the narrowest point of the Valley of Vermont. The area grew in economic importance with first, the discovery of marble and the opening of the **first marble quarry in the United States** near East Dorset in 1785. In the mid-nineteenth century, with the coming of the railroad, the valley entered a more industrial phase. Across U.S. 7 from the entrance to the park, a blast furnace was built in 1849 that was said to have had a capacity of 1,000 tons of iron per day. By 1889, however, the ore was exhausted.

The trail begins across from the park contact station. Walk up the grassy hill to a path along the back of the cemetery (Stop 1). The cemetery dates back to the

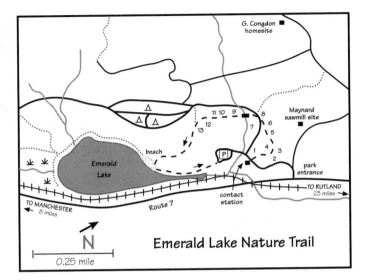

Emerald Lake Nature Trail

1830s and is in use today. If you are interested in local history, a brochure is available from the park ranger. Stop 2 provides a view north up the valley, with Dorset Peak (elev. 3,770 feet) in the Taconics on the left and Baker Peak (elev. 2,850 feet) in the Green Mountains on the right.

Stops 3 and 4 refer to the **field** and its inhabitants. It is being kept open by brush-hogging or burning every several years. When we saw it, it had been cut the previous fall, so it was low and grassy (see page 148). To settle here, inhabitants must be adapted to the extreme conditions of an open area: direct sun, alternating soaking and parching, heavy winds, snow cover, and deep

The Valley of Vermont at its narrowest: the Green Mountains are on the left and the Taconics on the right.

frost. At the same time, they prepare the soil for the next succession of plants by aerating it, enriching it with dead organic matter, and providing shade and protection for seeds to germinate.

If the field hasn't been cut, you might see **milkweed**—a plant whose stem extends underground and which grows a very deep tap root. It has adapted to dry conditions by storing water in the form of a milky liquid. Although it only lives for one season, it widely disperses its familiar seeds. It is almost impossible to eradicate it, because its roots spread underground, store starch, and form new buds. So deep are they that even if a field is plowed, the roots remain, and soon new plants emerge.

Grasshoppers, leafhoppers, caterpillars, and thousands more insects come to feast on the greenery and use its protection to go through their life cycle stages. Above ground, they provide food for **shrews,** which eat two to three times their own weight every day to stay active day and night and keep their little hearts pumping at 1,200 beats per minute! Both insects and seeds attract a large variety of birds, and they and the rodents provide food for **raptors,** while **turkey vultures** do the housekeeping.

From the field, turn left down a short road through the woods. Along it is a wonderland of wildflowers, ferns, shrubs, and fungi—a profusion of plants that thrive in the **sweeter soils** of the Valley of Vermont's limestone bedrock. Stop 5 indicates that the trees and new growth here are returning from abandoned pasture. Some of the old pasture **grasses** can still be seen among the vegetation.

Stop 6 represents an early stage of forest succession, with **paper birch, aspen,** and **white pine.** These species are all relatively intolerant of shade and can withstand direct sun and weather. The open roadway creates an edge habitat for birds. You may see or hear many of the same birds found in your yard—but also **indigo buntings** and a variety of **warblers.** Stop 7, across the road, is the stream.

Stop 8 along the road on the right is a typical **northern hardwood forest**—trees that can grow in the shade of others and eventually outlive or outcompete them. Once established, a climax forest remains until it is disturbed from the outside by an event such as hurricane, fire, disease epidemic, or extensive cutting. Up the road on the right is the Hiking Trail. Turn left across from it on the Nature Trail. Under the tree canopy, the leaf litter stays damp and shaded, a perfect environment for many ferns (Stop 9), including **maidenhair** (with its distinctive black divided stalk), **sensitive** (because it dies at the first touch of frost), **Christmas, lady,** and **interrupted.**

Ferns produce **spores** to reproduce, but different species do it differently. Some, like the **common polypody,** have spores on their leaflets that can be seen as small dark dots. Others, like **cinnamon fern** and **sensitive fern,** produce spore cases or capsules of spores on separate stems, called **fertile leaves.** The spore cases produced by cinnamon ferns are cinnamon-colored, while sensitive fern produces dark, beadlike capsules on a stem—a staple in the winter diet of **wild turkeys.**

Stops 10 and 11 are related. At Stop 10, there are three layers to the forest. The **canopy** formed by the crowns of trees, which catch direct sunlight while creating a cool, shady environment below. The **understory,** made up of trees and shrubs that either have been outcompeted or are shade-tolerant. Among them are **hornbeam, ironwood, mountain maple,** and **witch-hazel.** The lowest layer of the forest is **leaf litter**—a rich humus supporting shade-tolerant plants, ferns, mosses, lichens, fungi, and wildflowers, like **red trillium, hepatica,** and **herb-Robert.**

A few steps farther is a **hemlock forest,** with no understory and few if any ground plants. Hemlock needles are acidic and over many years create an environment around them that discourages the growth of other species. Once their boughs cut off the light, little else grows beneath them. The heavy cover provided by hemlock makes it a **deer wintering yard,** resulting in the park's being closed to winter recreational use. On the road, we found a small deer skull and spine, with other bones and hair scattered about. It may have succumbed to the harsh winter, or it may have been run to ground by dogs or **eastern coyotes.** As a point of interest, **whitetail deer** grow a winter coat of special hollow hairs, providing tremendous insulation; the same hollow-fiber principle is used for the synthetic pile materials in outdoor clothing.

Stop 12 draws attention to the fungi and bacteria that turn leaf litter and dead trees back into soil. On dead trees, look for **rusty-hoof fomes,** a fungus that looks like a horse's hoof growing out of the trunk. Stop 13 is at a living sugar maple with many cavities in it. Animals such as **squirrels, raccoons,** and **porcupines** use such cavities as nests. In the mid-nineteenth century, when most of Vermont's forests were cleared, the porcupine population declined. Its natural predator, the **fisher** (or **fisher-cat**), also declined, but because of its valuable fur, it was trapped to extinction in the state. As Vermont reforested, porcupines returned in full force, doing much damage to trees. The fisher was reintroduced in 1959 to protect the forests and has been successfully reestablished.

Although it is popularly believed that fishers kill porcupines by flipping them on their backs and attacking their bellies, studies of the secretive, nocturnal fisher show that it kills with bites to the porcupine's face, and then flips it over to feed on it. The number of fishers has increased now, but porcupines have again decreased. As a result, fishers hunt rabbits and domestic cats allowed to run at night.

Arriving back on the paved road, turn right to the shore of Emerald Lake and its beach area. The narrowness of the Valley of Vermont is striking when seen from here. You can loop back to the parking lot on the trail that follows the lake's outlet stream—the headwater of Otter Creek, which drains the valley to the north. Just south of the park, the Battenkill drains it to the south. On the walk back along the stream to the parking lot we saw a **spotted sandpiper,** who entertained us as it bobbed about on its spindly, widespread legs at the water's edge.

Grass

Grass is the most ubiquitous flowering plant on earth and the world's most important food source, since grains like wheat, corn, barley, and rice are all grass. In fact, one-half of the United States is covered by grass! As I looked out over the grassy field above the cemetery, I started wondering: How do grassy fields stay that way? The thousands of square miles of lawns I've mowed certainly had some weeds in them, but only a minuscule fraction of the plant kingdom and always the same old few.

If you've tried to dig up **sod** to make a garden, you'll guess one reason why: most of a grass plant grows low to or under the ground. It spreads by **rhizomes** growing sideways and forming nodes, where new shoots grow up. Nodes are so close to one another that other plants have a hard time getting started. The root system is so extensive that for some grasses, 90 percent of their weight is underground. In an often-cited study, a researcher grew a single rye plant in a greenhouse for

Mt. Dorset rises above the grassy field at Emerald Lake.

four months and then measured the combined length of its roots. The result: a phenomenal 387 miles! The sod formed by grass is nearly impenetrable to virtually all but a few specialized plants, like the old familiar **dandelion,** with its stout, downward-driving taproot that penetrates the sod and plunges into the soil beneath it.

If you were to mow a field of wildflowers, they wouldn't grow right back. Yet grass grows back after mowing. This is because grass, unlike most plants, doesn't grow from the tips of its leaves or shoots. They've adapted to mowing, drought, sunburn, and fire by having **growth tissue at the base of their stem.** People sometimes mistakenly think that tree branches get higher as a tree grows, but that's not so. If you were to drive a nail into a tree, it would never get higher. However, if you could drive a nail into a blade of grass, it would rise as the grass grew from its base.

The **grass family** has the third-largest number of species, surpassed only by the daisies and orchids. Among them are many old favorites: crabgrass, quack grass, tickle grass, and timothy grass. The giant of the family, however, is **elephant grass** (*Phragmites communis*). It can stand as tall as 13 feet, its soft plume (**inflorescence**) wafting in the wind. It is a true grass, not a rush, and fields of it can often be found where the ground is wet or marshy.

Getting There

Emerald Lake State Park is north of Manchester on US 7. Heading north out of East Dorset on US 7, the park is on the left at 3.6 miles.

Affiliated Organizations

Vermont Agency of Natural Resources, Department of Forests, Parks and Recreation (Pittsford office).

In the Area

A system of trails extends from the state park to the old country road, where the cellar holes of the homes of early inhabitants may be found. Beyond is the Texas marble quarry. North on the old country road is a spur trail to a natural stone bridge. A brochure available from the park ranger contains trail information and a map.

Hapgood Pond

Green Mountain National Forest, Peru

- **0.8 mile**
- **30–60 minutes**
- **very easy/easy (first portion wheelchair-accessible)**
- **entrance fee during the season**

A walk around a woodland pond through a variety of ecosystems. Benches are at scenic spots, and signs illustrate wildflowers.

The U.S. Forest Service purchased this land in 1931 — the first tract acquired to form the **Green Mountain National Forest** (which is now about 300,000 acres). For many years, the dam-formed pond was used to power mills. Hapgood Pond is stocked with **trout** and is popular for fishing. The area is operated by the Vermont Youth Conservation Corps under a special permit from the U.S. Forest Service. The Corps, a nonprofit organization funded by grants and donors, employs youths throughout Vermont. While visiting Hapgood, take time to talk to Corps members about this renowned education, conservation, and service organization.

We started at the picnic ground near the footbridge, where the trail is wide, graveled, and wheelchair-accessible. A **barrier-free fishing access** makes it easy to fish

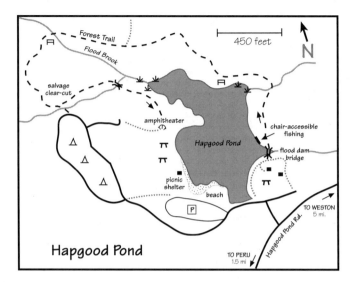

Hapgood Pond

from a wheelchair. It was established in 1990 by the Marble Valley Lions Club in cooperation with the U.S. Forest Service. As we passed over Flood Dam Bridge, I looked forward and back. The stream divides a much younger forest behind me from a mature and differently composed one in front.

The first of many wildflower illustration signs on the trail states, in part, "The signs on this trail have been created for those, like myself, who often find flowers in the woods and wonder about them, but never quite get around to looking them up. I have listed the food and medicinal uses as points of interest." It is signed by Lynn Moulton, 1994 Youth Corps Crew Member. Lynn draws and describes such wildflowers as **sarsaparilla, blue flag,** the **pink lady's-slipper** and **moccasin-flower orchids, winterberry, teaberry,** and **painted trillium.**

The trail climbs a small hill above the pond and passes through mixed evergreens, which give way to **yellow birch.** The pond is at an elevation of about 2,000 feet, and **black birch** doesn't commonly grow above 1,500 feet, so it's not likely to be found here.

The shallow water at the north end of the pond forms a **cattail marsh.** The trail continues undulating up and down. On the left is a large **beech tree** with **beech bark disease.** The disease begins when **scale insects** bore holes into beech bark, enabling a **fungus** to invade the tree. It is common throughout Vermont, and many

One of the most beautiful irises, the larger blue flag, grows in shallow water at the edge of the pond.

Cattails indicate a marsh or littoral zone of a lake or pond—an area that is slowly returning to dry land.

beeches are being harvested before the disease advances to the point where it destroys the value of the wood.

At a brook, we sat on the bench to enjoy the water's babbling and calls and songs of birds. We then meandered on the trail along the brook and its small floodplain—no surprise, since it is called **Flood Brook.** After crossing a bridge, we climbed to higher ground and followed the edge of a field full of stumps and mixed trees and shrubs. Clearly this area was recovering from a **clear-cut** (see next page). Past this area we came to an intersection. A right turn leads back to the campground, but we continued straight along the brook. At a low area where two brooks merge, the trail crosses a bridge and follows the stream bank. A large **speckled alder** and

red-osier dogwood thicket marks the lowlands where Flood Brook flows into Hapgood Pond. A stroll past the swimming area brought us back to the parking lot.

A Salvage Clear-Cut

Until several years ago, a tall stand of **Norway spruce** filled the area near Flood Brook. They were planted by the Civilian Conservation Corps about 60 years ago. In early October 1987, an unusual early storm brought not only high winds, but deep loads of wet, heavy snow. Many of the spruce blew over, while the weight of the snow broke the tops and boughs of those left standing. The trees could not be saved, and since they had been planted for sawlogs, there was little point in simply letting them die and decay.

The U.S. Forest Service decided to perform a **salvage clear-cut.** The trees were harvested to become wood products, while **early succession species** began regenerating. Below elevations of 2,500 feet, the climax of this cycle is usually a **hemlock/northern hardwood forest.** This type of forest covers almost 70 percent of Vermont's forested land.

Typical early succession species—**pin cherry** (sometimes called **fire cherry** because it quickly invades burnt-over areas), **quaking aspen, paper birch trees,** and **blackberries**—are thriving on this once clear-cut land. They grow fast but are short-lived. **Yellow birch, red maple,** and **beech** can also be seen growing among them. They will eventually become the predominant species. There is little commercial value to the early plants, but this diverse new growth provides protection and food for many species of birds and mammals. It also provides the protection from sun and wind needed by more valuable, shade-tolerant species to seed. For more on clear-cutting, see page 334.

Getting There
Hapgood Pond is just north of Peru, not far from the Bromley Mountain ski area. There are two turns off Route 11 that lead into Peru. Both are marked, and which you take depends on whether you are traveling east or west. They both lead shortly to the tiny village of Peru. Hapgood Pond Road begins across from the Peru Country Store. At 1.6 miles north on Hapgood Pond Road, the pond is on the left.

Affiliated Organizations
The Hapgood Pond Recreation Area is in the Green Mountain National Forest. It is operated by the Vermont Youth Conservation Corps under a special permit from the U.S. Forest Service.

In the Area
Nearby Bromley Mountain includes a stretch of the **Appalachian/Long Trail.** The three-mile (one-way) hike takes you to its 3,284-foot summit, with excellent views of Stratton and Equinox mountains. However, from Memorial Day to mid-October, you might also enjoy taking the ski lift to the top and coming down the country's first alpine slide.

White Rocks and Ice Beds
Green Mountain National Forest, near Wallingford

- 2-mile round-trip (0.5-mile round-trip to overlooks)
- 700 feet of ascent (400 foot elevation gain to overlooks)
- 1.5–3 hours (45 minutes)
- difficult/moderate
- entrance fee during the season
- bring binoculars and a camera, wear hiking boots

Dramatic views of huge boulder slides and of the Valley of Vermont. More descending and climbing brings you to the ice beds, where ice remains throughout the summer.

For the short climb to the overlooks, the results are spectacular. We left the western corner of the parking lot on the blue-blazed trail into the woods. Soon easy walking gave way to climbing, with rock forming portions of the trail. At one point, the trail appears to go straight up a rocky ridge, but it actually turns to the right to climb the western side.

The rocky rubble on either side of the trail begets an appreciation for the days of labor that went into constructing this trail. We then began a short but very steep climb that switches back and forth five times to gain elevation.

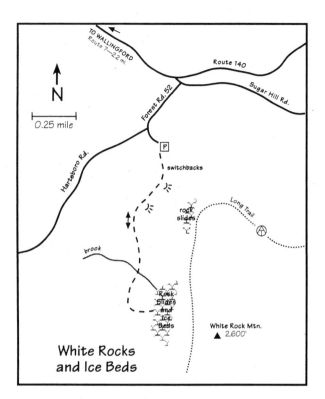

At the trail intersection on top, we turned left to an overlook and our first view of the white rock slides. Once we
caught our breath (by looking at the *breathtaking* view), we
returned to the intersection and continued straight.

The roots of the **white pines** and **hemlocks** growing here help to break up the rock. The extent to which
they noodle themselves into every crack and cranny—
and then thicken, widening the fissures in the stone—is

pretty spectacular along this portion of the trail. We were also tempted to stroke the beautiful gray-green patches of **rock spikemoss** that seem to carpet all surfaces. The spikemoss provides valuable clues about the rock itself (see page 162).

The trail does some zigzagging, properly double-blazed, and leads to a junction. By staying to our left, we came to the exposed ledge from which the views are even more dramatic than at the first lookout. The white rockfall is to the left; due south is the Valley of Vermont and US 7; and in the Taconics, on the right side of the valley, is the **talc mine** at South Wallingford. Vermont is one of the largest talc-producing states.

The White Rock cliffs were one of 27 documented locations in Vermont where **peregrine falcons** historically nested. For several years, the state released peregrines here in the hopes that they would reestablish nesting sites. According to Steve Parren, coordinator, Nongame and Natural Heritage, Vermont Fish and Wildlife Department, the attempts were probably unsuccessful because of the disturbance of so many visitors along the trail. Studies indicate that no matter how strongly worded the signs or how secure the barrier when a trail is temporarily closed, far too many people are undeterred. If you encounter requests to avoid areas to protect habitat, please respect them.

The rock here is covered with yellowish **map lichen,** a **crustose,** or crusty lichen (see page 300). There are also **crescentic fractures** (see page 71) in the rock, created as the glacier passed over here. As we examined them, Patti had a wonderful experience: a chickadee flew out from the trees and landed on her head. I love walking with her because she seems to attract wildlife as well as St. Francis of Assisi.

The white rocks below are at the end of the 0.75-mile walk down. Take into account that if you walk down 300 feet, you will have to climb back up 300 feet. If you are content with this distant view, you can return to the parking lot. If you are curious and your legs aren't tired, head on.

Return to the trail junction and continue on the **Ice Beds Trail.** If you look back, you can catch a good view to the north of the ledge you were just on. Soon the trail heads steeply downhill, with some poor footing. After a half-mile of descent, it levels out and joins a road, which crosses a brook twice. Test the water's temperature with your finger and see if you can guess the source of the water. After a short incline, we arrived at the base of the **Cheshire quartzite** rocks that slid off the cliffs and piled up at the bottom. **Cheshire** simply refers to one of many types of quartzite. (Geologic terms derive from places, generally the region where there is good evidence of something or where something was first discovered.)

Rock rubble piled at the base of a cliff such as this is called **talus;** the smaller stones and pebbles lying nearer the cliff at the top of the pile are called **scree.** The top of the slide is about 500 feet above you.

A U.S. Forest Service sign here reads:

A shattering of Cheshire quartzite rock probably occurred during the ice age to create this rock slide. During the winter, ice and snow accumulate in the depths of the rock crevices. A continual

One of several white rock slides of quartzite boulders. The ice caves are within the boulder talus.

downdraft of cold air in the shaded canyon helps preserve the ice and snow during the summer. The stream flowing from the rocks is fed by the melting ice. This keeps the water temperature at approximately 40 degrees throughout the summer.

Fitzhugh T. Lee studied this area for two years for the U.S. Geological Survey to learn more about the movement of the rocks on the slope above. His work indicates that though the glacier may have scoured the mountain and exposed the face of the quartzite, its subsequent fracturing and falling is the result of other natural processes.

The process begins with frost causing **microfractures** in the rock face. **Frost heave** then completes the fracture through the stone. Because quartzite is brittle and breaks cleanly along fracture lines, it doesn't form crevices where water can collect, freeze, and expand; once a fracture opens, water runs right down through it and escapes. However, when these fractures become dammed by ice and snow, ice contributes to the breakup. Once a layer of rock fractured, it slides down the slope and eventually tumbles to the bottom as a result of frost heave and loosening by **tree roots.**

From his measurements and judging by the small rockfall given the 10,000-year time period, Lee concluded that the process in this type of rock proceeds much more slowly than in other types. His calculations show that the rate the blocks on the cliff side are moving down the slope is a minimum of about six to eight inches every 1,000 years.

Rock Spikemoss

Soil changes can be deduced by observing which plants grow where. **Rock spikemoss** on the White Rocks trail is a good example of this type of natural interrelationship. Actually, it isn't in the moss family at all. The spikemosses have a quite different means of reproduction from mosses. It is much more highly developed and is, in fact, quite similar to that of coniferous trees. In any case, spikemoss loves an **acidic environment.** Thus, wherever you see it growing in large patches on rocks—identified by its gray-green color and smooth, low, velvety appearance—it is safe to assume that the rocks are acidic in nature.

The deep, plush gray-green mats of rock spikemoss.

Acidity in rocks derives from quartz. **Granite** is acidic because of its high quartz content. **Quartzite** has even more quartz in it than granite. If one knows that the origins of the Green Mountains were not volcanic (and thus not made of granite), the presence of spike-moss means that the rock must be a form of quartzite.

Quartzite is formed of **sandstone** that has under-gone sufficient heat and pressure to be changed (or **metamorphosed**) into quartzite. To figure out where sandstone comes from, a little background about how moving water and particles behave is necessary. Often there are rocks and boulders in streambeds. These are so heavy that they are only moved by the water during the most powerful floods. Small particles, on the other hand, can be carried easily by moving water. The faster water moves, the larger the particles (like **sand**) it can carry; conversely, when water moves slowly, it can only carry very tiny particles (**silt**).

During the spring runoff and floods, a river carries particles of many sizes. But when it hits the ocean, the movement of its waters gradually slow. When it begins to slow, it drops its larger particles first. Thus, sand accumulates near its mouth, sometimes forming deltas. The water finally comes to rest farther out in the ocean, where it drops its smallest particles, silt—which become clay. Sands are found near the edge of a continent and clays are found farther offshore.

Over the millenia, layers of sediment build up miles thick. This creates heat and pressure, which changes **sand** into **sandstone** and **clay** into **shale** (and maybe eventually **slate**). If additional heat and pressure are added to the sandstone, it becomes **quartzite.** Thus, the rock spikemoss here means that several hundred million years ago, this mountain began as sand at the bottom of the shallow sea just off the continental coast.

Getting There

White Rocks is southeast of Wallingford off Route 140. From the intersection of US 7 and Route 140, turn east on Route 140. At 2.2 miles, turn right onto Sugar Hill Road. In several hundred yards, turn right at the sign for the USFS White Rocks Picnic Area.

Affiliated Organizations

The White Rocks Picnic Area is in the Green Mountain National Forest, managed by the U.S. Forest Service.

Big Trees Nature Trail
Lake St. Catherine State Park

- **1 mile total**
- **45–60 minutes**
- **easy**

This is a very pleasant 0.3-mile ridge walk to see large trees and a variety of wildflowers and shrubs. From there, the 0.75-mile Hiking Trail is an easy walk through an overgrown meadow full of birds.

A split-rail fence at the park entrance is made of **black locust.** Nothing surpasses locust for long-lived fence posts, especially when the end in the ground is the one that was oriented upward in the tree. This prevents the cells that move water up the tree (by capillary action) from drawing moisture from the ground. Black locust has a thick, sharply tapering trunk, extremely deep bark furrows, and relatively short, curving, heavy, thorned branches. When you see a row of them along the drive to an old farmhouse, they make an impressive sight indeed.

The trail begins just inside the park on the right, next to the woodshed, and starts by running parallel to the park access road. Stop 1 is the Vermont state tree— **sugar maple** (also called **hard maple** or **rock maple**). Today it is the single most economically important tree in the state. Of course it provides maple sugar—about a half-million gallons annually, for which Vermont is just-

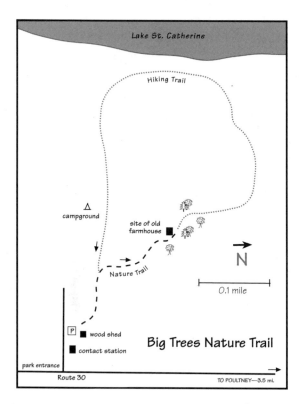

Lake St. Catherine

Hiking Trail

△ campground

site of old farmhouse

Nature Trail

N

0.1 mile

P ■ wood shed

■ contact station

Big Trees Nature Trail

park entrance

Route 30

TO POULTNEY—3.5 mi.

ly famous—and it provides hard maple lumber for furniture and fine woodworking. But as Charles Sprague Sargent wrote in 1890, "Much of the splendor of the northern forest in early autumn is due to the abundance of the Sugar Maple, which is then unsurpassed in brilliancy of color by any upland tree." It is to see that splendor that visitors travel to Vermont from the world over every October. Thus sugar maple makes a major contribution to the state's largest industry — tourism.

Stop 2 is a **white ash.** Its distinctive diamond-furrowed bark makes it relatively easy to identify. To confirm its identity, look up at its branches: pairs of stout twigs grow out of a branch directly across from each other (**opposite branching**). The only other full-grown trees with opposite branching are the maples, but maple's long, slender twigs are distinctly different from the short, stout ones of ash.

You'll find a **shagbark hickory** at Stop 3 — a tree whose name provides an obvious clue to recognizing it. The shreds of bark coming off the tree vertically begin to form when the tree is about 40 years old. Its roasted nuts (and those of **butternut** trees) were an early American snack food, and their husks were crushed and thrown in the water to poison fish. Whatever the chemical mechanism, it didn't affect the edibility of the fish that floated to the top for easy gathering. This practice has since been outlawed.

Many of the trees along the trail are covered by **wild grapevine.** It climbs by means of its **tendrils** and spreads over the tree's crown. When it unrolls its large leaves, it steals sunlight from the tree, weakening or killing it. It also forms a thick mat that collects snow, causing breakage in the branches. Several dead trees killed by grapevine can be seen along the trail with the vines still on them. If you're lost in the woods and thirsty, you can cut a grapevine and drink the cool, clear sap that runs out. If you love trees, grapevine is an enemy; if you love birds, wild grape is a friend, since its fruit — sweetened after the first frost — draws them from far and wide.

Stop 4 is the highly prized **black cherry,** whose bark looks as if the tree were covered with burnt potato chips. The aroma of its bark and twigs is reminiscent of bitter almond. Traces of hydrocyanic acid are found in its bark, leaves, and cherry pits, though it is only potentially harmful in very large quantities.

After this stop, the trail turns right at the yellow arrow and from here on is marked by blue blazes. It then climbs to the top of a small ridge and follows it for some distance. Stop 5 marks several large **eastern white pine** trees (see page 9). Stop 6 is a **butternut** tree (see page 244 and page 290), and Stop 7 is an **American basswood** (or **linden**) tree. It is considered a hardwood, though its wood is very soft and much used by wood carvers. Without getting technical, **hardwood** refers to **deciduous** trees, while **softwood** refers to **coniferous** trees. The terms do not necessarily describe the wood, however, because many softwoods have harder wood than many hardwoods, and vice versa.

Stop 8 is **ironwood** (or **musclewood**). In Ledges Overlook (page 90), we discuss at length the confusion over the name of this tree—though there's no quibbling with the fact that musclewood is the most descriptive of the tree's form. Just before Stop 9 is a large, spreading **northern red oak** (Stop 11 is another red oak). I measured this tree's diameter in early 1995 at almost precisely 48 inches. Big as it is though, it falls far short of the largest red oaks in Vermont. According to the 1994 biannual list of the state's largest trees, there is one in Hubbardton that measures 76 inches (more than six feet) in diameter.

Stop 9 is **eastern hemlock,** a tree whose bark has provided **tannin** for tanning leather, but whose lumber

From little acorns do mighty oaks grow—as did this northern red oak along the Big Trees Nature Trail.

has never been really prized because it is subject to **shakes** (the separation of annual rings caused by wind and trunk sway). Farmers often send hemlock to the mill for construction lumber to build outbuildings. Pound a nail into green hemlock and it will shrink around it so tightly as the wood seasons that it can't be pulled out again. The commercial forest products industry, however, shuns hemlock and depends primarily upon white pine, spruce, and fir. Hemlock is an aesthetic favorite of many people for its stately shape and delicate foliage.

It is pretty easy to spot a hemlock from afar: it's the tree whose leaders at the top droop over. In *Tall Trees, Tough Men* (a book I highly recommend), Robert Pike recounts how loggers used to find their way in the forest by relying on hemlock leaders that invariably drooped to the east. After examining a number of my hemlock trees, I decided that if I used that piece of folk wisdom to find my way, I'd still be walking in circles. Of course, maybe those wise, old-growth hemlocks were smarter than my young upstarts.

The trail then bears to the right with a berry patch on the left. Stop 10 is a **domestic apple** tree gone wild. It is a favorite of deer and other wildlife, who serve as vehicles for transporting its seeds after eating an apple, core and all. Stop 11 is the red oak (see page 185).

The Nature Trail ends at Stop 12, **the old farmstead.** The steps and foundation remain and there are views of the Taconic Mountains and Lake St. Catherine. To return, retrace your steps, or you can continue, as we did, on the Hiking Trail. Following the sign, we started downhill on a trail covered by pine needles. On the right were more remains of the old farm, including a bathtub.

We continued on, heading gradually downhill on a lovely path through the woods. Several **American elm** line the path as it follows the edge of a field and a stand of pine. We passed another large basswood tree and then switched back to complete the descent, which took us into a field of grasses, brambles, and berries. On the left were several **tamarack (American larch)** trees and on the right, a row of **spruce trees** that were being attacked by spruce galls. **Alder, dogwood, sensitive** and **lady ferns, meadow fescue,** and a hundred other species expressing life's natural exuberance under the sun, combined to leave me with the impression that this was once a wetter area than it is today.

On this fine spring day, we flushed out songbirds with every step, walked through a berry patch upon which those birds will no doubt be feasting later in the summer, passed by a lazy willow, and stepped carefully so as not to squash the violets. It was a beautiful, quiet walk through a very large and open meadow, eventually joining the Big Trees Nature Trail, which we followed back to our car.

Tamarack *(American Larch or Hackmatack)*

When you come to the tamaracks in the field on this walk, it is worth the few steps to take a closer look at them. Tamarack grows farther north than any other

A tamarack in spring shows the openness of its foliage.

North American tree. Look how randomly their short, light-green needles seem to grow out from the branches. This gives tamarack a look that is lighter and more open than other evergreens, but it doesn't grow that way for aesthetic reasons. In the far north, where sunlight is at a premium for much of the year, its rays pass through the tamarack's boughs down to its bottom branches, enabling it to catch more sunlight.

To adapt to the land of the midnight sun, it drops its needles to conserve energy through the six months of darkness—the only conifer to do so. Tamarack loves marshy, quaky areas and bogs. There, once its needles have dropped, it fools the unsuspecting into thinking it is a dead pine tree that has succumbed to the overly wet conditions. But come spring, when its new needles emerge, it is one of the most beautiful of trees, especially if you catch it with the sunlight filtering through its boughs and misty, lime-green needles early in the morning.

Getting There

Lake St. Catherine State Park is on Route 30, southeast of Poultney. Take Route 30 south out of Poultney and the park entrance is on your right in 3.5 miles.

Affiliated Organizations

Vermont Agency of Natural Resources, Department of Forests, Parks and Recreation (Pittsford office).

Rutland Area

Slate History Trail
Bomoseen State Park

- **0.75 mile**
- **1 hour**
- **very easy**

A short, level, road walk around abandoned West Castleton and its slate industry sites — easy walking and visually and historically fascinating.

For a change of pace, stroll through a village that is no more. Only stone is left: the slate that drew people here from as far as Europe. A quirk in the cataclysmic Taconic mountain-building a half-billion years ago begins a story that continues today (see page 114).

If you are staying at or visiting Bomoseen State Park, walk out the entrance. Otherwise, pull off the road across from Stop 2. At this stop is a pile of **slate rubble,** the first of many vestiges left by the once-thriving community. In the mid-1800s, West Castleton was a bustling crossroads, a company town crowded with immigrant workers who labored in its busy quarries and slate mills. Today it is silent, except for those here to enjoy the lakeside recreation.

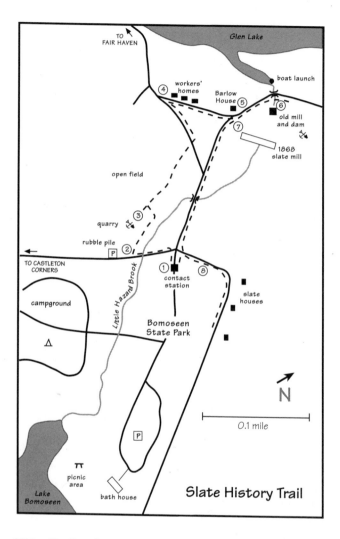

TO
FAIR HAVEN

Glen Lake

boat launch

workers'
homes

④

Barlow
House

⑤

⑥

old mill
and dam

⑦

1868
slate mill

open field

quarry

③

rubble pile

P

②

TO CASTLETON
CORNERS

①

contact
station

⑧

slate
houses

Little Hazard Brook

campground

Bomoseen
State Park

△

N

0.1 mile

P

picnic
area

bath house

Lake
Bomoseen

Slate History Trail

Only about 15 percent of quarried slate is usable, accounting for the huge rubble pile. Of the three slate belts in Vermont, the Castleton area was the most profitable. It produced **purple** and **unfading green slate,** seen here in the rubble and on the slate roofs in Castleton and Fair Haven. (We chose green Vermont slate tiles from a quarry in this region for our living room floor. It's easy to clean, doesn't wear out, is fireproof around the wood-burning stove, provides a passive solar heat sink, and makes a beautiful background for a handwoven wool rag rug my parents made 40 years ago.)

Up the old road, we turned left to Stop 3, where a spur to the left leads to the **quarry**—one of more than 100 working in the area in the 1880s. The double stacks of slate are called **deadmen** and were used to anchor the derricks and pulleys that hoisted slate blocks from the depths of the quarry, now filled with water. Slate is heavy, and transportation costs impose a limit on its market. In 1852, when the West Castleton Railroad and Slate Company came to West Castleton, it was a tremendous boon. By 1854, there were 25 slate quarries in the area employing 800 men. Laborers of the time worked a 10-hour day for less than two dollars. In times of cash shortages, like the Civil War, workers were issued scrip, good at the company store.

From the quarry, we walked across the field and turned left on the paved road to Stop 4, the **workers' homes.** Only several foundations are left of the nearly 20 homes and tenements that originally lined both sides of the road. Each foundation supported a wood-framed house divided into two small residences. Compare the space in which these immigrant families, mostly Irish

Catholic, lived to what we and our children enjoy today.

Down the road on the left is the beautiful **Barlow House** (Stop 5), built about 1900 on the foundation of one of the workers' homes. It houses a **slate museum.** Up the road to our left, at the corner of the boat launch access road, are a **shagbark hickory** and a **red oak** tree growing together—an unusual combination in Vermont. They are a prelude to the oak/hickory forest on the Glen Lake Trail three miles north.

The finger of water at the boat launch is not on nineteenth-century maps, when Little Hazard Brook flowed from Glen Lake near the Barlow House. Its course was changed when a dam was built to increase

A small slate museum is located in Barlow House. Its roof, chimney, and retaining wall are all slate.

the headwaters driving the mill's water-wheel. The mill (Stop 6) sawed both lumber and slate.

We walked back on the road, turned left, and came to the 1868 slate mill on the corner (Stop 7). It is so over-grown now that it looks like a set from *Raiders of the Lost Ark*. It was built to prepare slate flooring, billiard tables, sinks, and washtubs. At 64 feet wide by 265 feet long, it was one of the largest slate finishing mills in the country. **Slate marbleizing,** which produced imitation marble— was also done here, making it possible for common hous-es to have mantles that looked like those in the great homes. The mill was powered by a 24-foot-diameter water wheel, which drove all its equipment. When it burned in 1870, it was rebuilt on a smaller scale. Its con-stuction date, beautifully carved in stone over the door-

The facade of the slate mill originally built in 1868.

way, remains, but the walls are crumbling, and you are asked not to climb on the foundation. We especially liked the rough slate and grass walk leading up to the mill.

Returning to the park entrance, we turned left to see the stacked-slate houses. Two of the three houses — dating from the 1880s — are now preserved as private residences. The middle house is owned by the state. The house on the left was the company office, store, and post office. The bell in front signaled starting and quitting times at the mill and quarries. You are asked to simply observe the houses from the road.

And that concludes the Slate History Trail.

The History of Vermont Slate

Lake Bomoseen is on the eastern edge of the Taconic Mountains at the north end of the Valley of Vermont. The slate began as deep sea sediments on the continental shelf, which began where eastern Vermont is today. When the continents drifted together, the sediments were pushed up and over the edge of the continent to become the Taconic Mountains. Under tremendous heat and pressure, some of the shale metamorphosed into slate and ended up in the region of Castleton, Hubbardton, Sudbury, Fair Haven, Poultney, and Wells. (At the same time, limestone metamorphosed into marble.) For more on the geology of this area, see Prospect Rock (page 114) and White Rocks (page 157).

Small-scale quarrying of slate roof shingles had occurred since the early 1700s, but Colonel Alonson Allen and Caleb Ranney were the first to quarry slate in the Castleton area. In 1839, they began working a ledge by hand near Ranney's home in Fair Haven. They hoped to produce school slates, but the slate was too hard, so they turned to providing hearths and tombstones. In 1848, the first barn was built with a slate roof. It still stands a mile south of Fair Haven on Route 22A. In Brattleboro, one of the most ambitious slate shingling projects probably ever attempted—the roofing and siding of seven huge Estey Organ factory buildings—began in 1870. It required about 100,000 square feet of slate shingles (in roofer's parlance, a thousand squares)! The complex was listed on the **National Register of Historic Places** in 1980.

Small-time slate production continued until the 1850s, when it rapidly expanded with the coming of the railroad and a source of skilled workers from Wales and Ireland. Although Irish Catholics came to Castleton, skilled workers from Wales provided most of the labor throughout the region. This region remains the most dense concentration of Welsh descendants in the United States. A collection of **Welsh Americana** is housed at the Green Mountain College in Poultney.

Vermont has always remained a strong second to Pennsylvania in slate production. Slate has been replaced by other materials for many uses, but the huge amounts of rubble remain. Red slate occurs only on the New York State side of the border, and recently a new use for its red rubble appeared; it is being ground up to use in tennis court surfaces. The thousands of tons of remaining rubble may one day become important as sources of aluminum oxide and bauxite.

Getting There

From the intersection of Routes 4A and 30 in Castleton Corners, go west on Route 4A. At 1.3 miles, turn right at the sign for Lake Bomoseen, West Shore. Stay to the right, and at 5.4 miles, bear right to Lake Bomoseen State Park.

Affiliated Organizations

Vermont Agency of Natural Resources, Department of Forests, Parks and Recreation (Pittsford office).

In the Area

A map for a driving tour to see slate roofs, sidewalks, and tombstones is available at the Bomoseen Nature Center or from the Vermont Division for Historic Preservation.

A one-hour, 1.5-mile hiking loop begins in the meadow behind the Lake Bomoseen State Park contact station. It leads through woods to a pleasant vista of Glen Lake.

The Glen Lake Trail connects Lake Bomoseen with Half Moon Pond. It is a 4.5-mile, one-way trail along the lake shore, past several marshes, and through forest. The Glen Lake Trail in this book describes a portion of the trail that passes through an oak/hickory forest.

Glen Lake Trail
Half Moon State Park

- **2 miles, steep up and down in places**
- **1.5–2 hours**
- **difficult**
- **bring binoculars, wear hiking boots**

This rugged trail in an area of geologic thrust faults leads through a beautiful woodland savannah and an oak/hickory forest to a remote marshland.

The 4.5-mile Glen Lake Trail connects the campgrounds at Half Moon State Park and Lake Bomoseen State Park (see Slate History, page 173). This walk is a one-mile section of that trail that starts near its northern terminus. Walk in through a stand of white pines following blue blazes. Continue past a clump of **northern white cedar.** These are the only white cedar to be seen on all of the walks in this book. It occurs in southern Vermont, but it becomes much more prominent in the north. Its common name is *arbor vitae,* the tree of life. You can believe that it acquired this name because it lives to be 200 to 300 years old or because it saved the men of Jacques Cartier's Canadian expedition, probably from scurvy.

The trail then enters a long stretch of **woodland savannah** composed of **hornbeam** and other species of young trees. This forest type stretches for some distance along the trail and brook. A savannah has a green forest

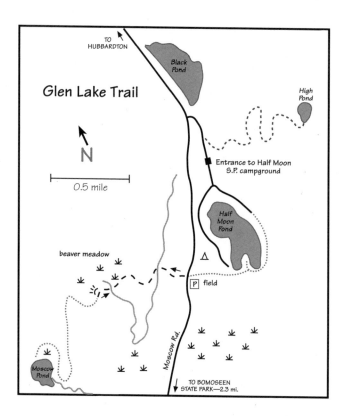

floor and lacks an understory. It is a beautiful, sunny green place, contrasting with the deep shade of forests. Here **sedges, princess pine,** and **star moss** carpet the forest. Sedges look like grasses, but their stems are triangular, not round. Remember: *Sedges have edges.*

The trail then begins to pass over a series of steep ridges. We are walking on the **frontal thrust fault zone** of the eastern edge of the Taconic Range. When the forces of the continental collision pushed against layers of rock, harder surface rocks simply thrust upward, rather than folding or bending (which is what the more fluid rocks deep in the earth did). A **thrust fault** resulted when thin slices of rock were pushed up over one another. Frontal thrust faulting occurred after the Taconic Range was built and is a much smaller, more local phenomenon. The eastern direction from which the force was applied is clearly deduced from the north-south orientation of the ridges and the angles of the exposed rock of the thrust plate.

There is a moderately difficult stream crossing between two of the ridges, at least depending on the height of the water. We passed a **basswood** tree with the sapsucker's characteristic horizontal rows of small holes. The **sapsucker** usually makes the holes and then goes on about his business. Sap fills the holes, and insects come to feed at the well. The sapsucker returns later for a feast of ants in sap sauce. Hummingbirds also depend on the holes, and thus migrate at the same time as the sapsuckers.

After the second ridge, **shagbark hickories** appear among the **red oaks.** This atypical section of forest is called an **oak/hickory forest** (see page 185). Notice that the oaks and hickories tend not to grow at the bottom of the ravines formed by the ridges, where the soil is wetter. After passing an outcropping of broken rock, the trail switches back hard to the right. The blazing here follows the principle I prefer: only one blazed tree at a time can be seen ahead. However, it means you must pay close attention, especially in areas like this, where the footpath is not always obvious. If you can't see a blaze, immedi-

Beaver meadow on the northern stretch of the Glen Lake Trail.

ately stop and retrace your steps to the last blaze. Stand there and look around until you spot the next one. If you're distracted and continue walking without keeping track of them, it is very easy to wander from the trail.

After climbing and descending the second ridge, the trail again crosses a small stream and starts up the next ridge, and so on. A sapsucker broke the law at a pine: he made a *vertical* row of holes following a seam in the bark. Throughout the walk, **wintergreen** can be found. It loves the acidic soil beneath oaks, and I love to snack on their small, red, mint-flavored berries, though it takes a while to gather a handful.

If you haven't given up by now because of the difficult footing (Patti did, so it's okay), you will soon arrive at Beaver Meadow. The trail comes out on a small ledge overlooking the large area. Sit there quietly and enjoy being so far from man-made sounds. This place has a wonderful sense of wildness about it, of the primeval, and from this vantage point, you can sit and enjoy it from a dry spot.

It is beautiful and secluded, making it is easy to spend time with so much activity and so many birds to watch in the marsh. Type A personalities, however, will probably start to return when the anxiety of sitting still overtakes them. Type B personalities may have to force themselves to leave before the sun sets. You retrace your steps, but be sure to spot each blaze ahead. On my return, I found a large area of forest floor scratched by a **wild turkey** in search of food.

Oak/Hickory Forests

It was much warmer in Vermont about 4,000 years ago, and oak, pine, and hickory, as well as many other warm-climate species, became common. Then, as the weather cooled back down, most of them retreated. However, pockets of a few species remained here. These pockets are called **relics.** The oak/hickory forests—primarily in Rutland and Addison counties—are relics of that period, as are the black gum trees in the Black Gum Swamp (page 39).

The nuts and acorns of an oak/hickory forest provide a rich diet for many animals. The quantities of seed produced by oaks and hickories vary from year to year, and the populations of wildlife rise and fall with the changes in their food supply. What is also curious is that the oaks and hickories are in tune: lean years are lean for both species. This type of forest is dominant around Boston but is not typical of Vermont. The pre-

The bark of a shagbark hickory begins peeling vertically as the tree matures.

mier oak/hickory forest in North America is right at the western limit of where deciduous trees dominate—in the Ozark highlands. Its topography consists of ridges and broken terrain, much like this stretch of the Glen Lake Trail.

Another factor in the ecology of oak/hickory forests is the leaf litter. **Northern red oak** contributes to the acidity of the soil, but on top of that, the nutrients in the leaf return into the tree's branches before the leaf falls from the tree. What little nutrition remains, the oak reclaims, so there is seldom an abundance of plants and wildflowers where it grows. Wintergreen, however, proliferates under red oak trees.

Both trees have adapted by developing large seeds. When their nuts germinate, they put out a stout root that is able to penetrate the thick, leathery leaf litter above the ground. At the same time, the large nut meat provides nourishment for the seedling to get established.

Getting There

Near the Lake Bomoseen State Park entrance (see Slate History Trail), a sign directs you to Half Moon State Park (which offers no day use, only overnight camping). Moscow Road leads to Half Moon. Take it 3 miles north. At the first open meadow on the right, there are fence posts whose tops are painted blue and a sign points to Half Moon. Park well off the road on the shoulder and look for the trail into the woods on the other side of the road from the meadow. A brown-and-white sign, set back about 20 feet along the trail in the pines, reads "Glen Lake Trail, Vermont Youth Corps, 1987."

Affiliated Organizations

Vermont Agency of Natural Resources, Department of Forests, Parks and Recreation (Pittsford office).

In the Area

There is a short trail to High Pond from Half Moon Park. It can be reached from an old woods road off the access road to the park or — via a connector trail — from the short walk around the pond. The Slate History Trail and a small slate museum are located at Lake Bomoseen State Park, 3.5 miles south on the Moscow Road.

Gifford Woods
Gifford Woods State Park

- no formal trail; wander through a deciduous old-growth forest
- 30 minutes
- easy
- bring binoculars and a camera

*A walk through Gifford Woods affords a rare and unique
experience of an old-growth virgin hardwood forest.*

Park near the road at the fishing access to Kent Pond. If
you look on both sides of the parking lot, you will see the
telltale white blazes of the **Appalachian Trail,** which cuts
through Gifford Woods State Park on the other side of
the road. Walk to the road and turn right, and in a short
distance you'll see the old trees and informal paths into
the woods. (If you enter and park at the state park, simply walk directly across the road and into the woods.)

Most of the trees here are **sugar maples,** but among
them are old-growth **yellow birch, beech, basswood,
white ash,** and **hemlock.** The understory is rich with
native wildflowers growing in the deep fertile soil. The
trees branch high off the ground, and their heavy
gnarled branches speak more of their age than any
other feature. One needs binoculars to discern the
leaves far above to determine identity, because the bark

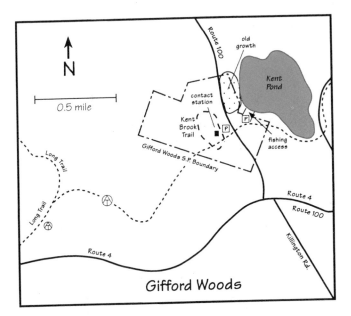

Gifford Woods

on the trunks of these ancient trees tends to look the same from species to species. Some of these trees have been dated at more than 400 years old—their seeds germinating at about the time Columbus set sail.

Trees have been my most important teachers in life. These wise old trees remind me of two of their most important lessons. First, a tree's youth is not merely a memory. Every year of its existence is part of the structure that is before you today. Its early years as a sapling still exist, and are called, for good reason, *heart*wood.

The second lesson is that a tree, to survive, must grow in two directions. If it only tries to rise above its neighbors and grow upward to be in the spotlight, so to speak, it blows over in the first high wind. At the same time that it seeks the light, its roots must grow downward. In the inner dark world of the earth, they must extend toward the center and expand to match the spreading branches above. Perhaps these trees may speak to you of their centuries of trials and the strength they have developed to withstand all setbacks.

Gifford Woods extends for only about seven acres between the road and Kent Pond, but has been much visited and studied. It was designated a **National Natural Landmark** in 1980 and a **State Fragile Area** in 1982.

The bole of a 400-year-old sugar maple.

How Trees Grow

A tree can be seen as an **energy system.** The source of its energy is the sun and nutrients in the ground. Given a finite amount of energy, it must *decide* how to spend it. First, it uses energy to **put out leaves** each spring. The fact that evergreens stay green year-round — saving them the energy of putting out new leaves each spring and providing them with continuous energy from the sun — enables them to live in more extreme climates. That's why the boreal forest is composed almost exclusively of evergreens (see High Country, page 199).

The second demand on its energy is to **grow tall and spread its crown and root system.** This is necessary to its survival. A forest can be seen as simply a bunch of trees trying to kill each other (it's a *tree-eat-tree world* out there in the woods). When a tree gets a slight edge over its neighbors, it gets more of the sun's energy and can spread its crown to become a dominant tree.

After growing leaves and growing taller, a tree then turns to **putting out seed.** This ensures the survival of the species. Lastly, with whatever energy might be left, it puts on **girth.** A tree that must compete vigorously will have little energy left, and its annual rings will be very close together. Thus, girth alone doesn't reflect a tree's age. While these old-growth trees have to use most of their energy to grow taller and spread their branches within the confines of their neighbors, dooryard and fencerow trees that grow in full sunlight manage their energy in a different way. From the time they are young saplings, they have the luxury of easily spreading their crowns in all directions, increasing their energy from the sun without having to stretch heavenward. They get so

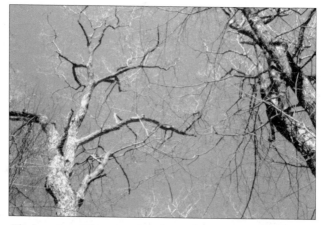

The branches of these trees have borne the weight of every snowfall and ice storm since before the time of European exploration of Vermont.

much energy from their huge crowns that they have plenty left over to put on substantial girth.

You can see that while many of the sugar maples in Gifford Woods are around 400 years old, they are only four feet or so in diameter. By contrast, the Vermont champion sugar maple grew in the open and may be as young as 150 years old, but its diameter is more than five and a half feet. It's an entirely different shape as well. Its crown has spread 88 feet, which is also its height—it's as wide as it is tall! These old-growth trees, on the other hand, had their crowns restricted by competition and used much of their limited energy to put out leaves and seeds and to grow taller, rather than increasing their girth. Thus, old doesn't necessarily mean big.

Many popular guides to tree identification present drawings of tree silhouettes as an aid. Unfortunately, they always show open-grown tree shapes that bear little if any resemblance to trees growing in a forest. Once you leave your lawn, you're out of luck trying to use them.

Getting There

Gifford Woods State Park is located on Route 100, just north of Killington. Go north 0.4 mile on Route 100 from its intersection with US 4, across from the Killington Road. Pull into the access to Kent Pond on the right, or continue 0.1 mile and turn left into the entrance of Gifford Woods State Park.

Affiliated Organizations

Vermont Agency of Natural Resources, Department of Forests, Parks and Recreation (Pittsford office).

In the Area

Several walks and hikes can be taken from the park. **The Kent Brook Trail** is a short, 0.5-mile nature trail that starts at the parking lot near the contact station and follows the perimeter of the park. More ambitious hikes can be taken on the **Appalachian Trail,** which runs through the park and joins the **Long Trail,** which runs north-south the length of Vermont, just 1.5 miles away. Maps are available from the park ranger.

Across US 4 is the access road to **Killington,** whose mountaintop trailheads can be reached by chairlift (see next page). You can also walk at Canfield-Fisher and Hurricane Forest to see giant old-growth white pine.

High Country Trail
Killington Resort, Merrell Hiking Center

- **3.2 miles, ride the chairlift up and descend 2,650 feet**
- **2–2.5 hours**
- **moderate/difficult**
- **fees for chairlift and guided walks; guidebook and map may be purchased**
- **bring binoculars, jacket, and hiking boots (boots may be rented at the hiking center)**

Here's a switch: start on a mountaintop and hike down, guided either by a trained naturalist or by a 50-page detailed guide and beautiful, information-packed map.

Most of the trails in this book take you *across* the landscape, while the trails at Killington provide a totally different experience: they take you *vertically* through the landscape. Of the many trails offered at Killington, we've selected the High Country Trail, since it is the shortest one with the most interest that takes you through four of Killington's six life zones: **arctic/alpine** on the summit, **spruce/fir, upper transition,** and **northern hardwoods.** As you approach Killington by car, you drive through the other two zones: a **floodplain** zone on U.S. 4 along the Ottauquechee River and the **lower**

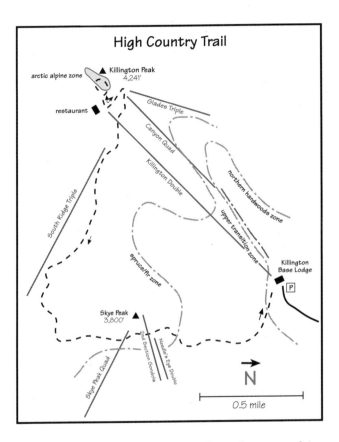

High Country Trail

- arctic alpine zone
- ▲ Killington Peak 4,241'
- Glades Triple
- restaurant
- Canyon Quad
- Killington Double
- northern hardwoods zone
- South Ridge Triple
- Upper transition zone
- spruce/fir zone
- Killington Base Lodge
- P
- Skye Peak ▲ 3,800'
- 2nd Section Gondola
- Needle's Eye Double
- Skye Peak Quad
- N
- 0.5 mile

transition zone, which you pass through as you drive up to the Killington Base Lodge.

The first three zones occur at elevations ranging from 2,500 feet to above 4,200 feet. The Killington Base Lodge, at 2,540-feet elevation, is already higher than any trail in this book. From there, the double chairlift rises to near the peak. For a *moderate* version of the walk, you can walk the first loop around the arctic/alpine zone, and then, for an additional fee, ride the lift back down.

When you get off the chairlift, follow the green number "1" on white signs straight ahead. If the weather is severe, avoid the summit loop. Remember that traveling vertically takes you through different climates. There is a temperature change, on average, of about 10°F per every 1,000 feet. Thus, the summit of Killington can be 25°F to 35°F cooler than where your day may have started. Above 4,000 feet, spring can come as much as two months later than in the river valleys.

Pick up the trail at Stop 1H, to the left of the chairlift, just across the chairlift line from the Peak Restaurant (from whose rooftop five states and Canada are visible). Generally, if the lifts are working, the restaurant is open, but check first at the Base Lodge if you plan to eat there or fill your water bottle. In the winter, the temperature can be as low as -35°F, with winds gusting to 70 MPH, and we are at the very upper range of where trees have adapted to survive. The paper birch you see at Stop 1A is not the same as paper birch at lower elevations. Some consider it a separate species— *Betula cordafolia*—while others consider it a variation of paper birch—*Betula papyrifera*. Its popular name is **heartleaf paper birch.**

We are in the upper reaches of a **boreal** or **spruce/fir forest. Red spruce** is rare above 3,700 feet, so the only tree is **balsam fir.** It protects itself from the drying effect of winds with a waxy coating on its needles, which is why it does so well indoors at Christmas. Its tapering

Red spruce can be found up to about 3,700 feet elevation. Its cones hang downward from the branches.

trunk and branches and flexible twigs, branches, and needles help it manage heavy snowfall and the weight of **rime ice** (the ice buildup from moisture in clouds).

On a clear day, several of the Green Mountains and Mt. Equinox in the Taconic Range can be seen from Stop 1D. To the west are the Adirondack Mountains. The stunted fir trees here are called **krummholz,** meaning crooked wood. The direction of their branches, like a weather vane, reflects the direction of the prevailing winds. The bare rock at Stop 1E is in the **arctic/alpine zone.** However, the zone here is too small to support typical alpine species. Lichens, however, are undeterred, and several species grow here, among them, yellowish-green **map lichens** (see Gordon Welchman, page 300).

At Stop 1H, David Laing, Killington staff naturalist, advises you to keep an eye out for the **yellow-rumped** or **myrtle warbler,** who nests here in the summer. Growing across the ski trail is mountain **shadbush,** a **Juneberry,** whose fruit is savored by **rose-breasted grosbeaks, robins,** and **hikers** — that is, if David himself has left any berries for others. The changing elevations provide a good opportunity to listen for thrushes (see Fort Dummer, page 57). In the upper transition region, you are likely to hear (and hopefully see) many warblers, including blackpolls, **black-and-whites, black-throated blues,** and **black-throated greens. Winter wrens** tend to stay at the high elevations as well, and **juncos** are common everywhere.

At the top of the Glades chairlift, you no longer follow the "1" signs; cut off to the right and follow the "2" signs. At Stop 2A is a fir trunk covered with **old-man's beard.** Although it looks like Spanish moss, it is, in fact, a **lichen.** Spanish moss, a member of the pineapple family, is a tropical plant. Both, however, are **epiphytes,** plants that grow on other plants without harming them.

The trail then begins its steep descent, and with the above, we hope to have given you the flavor of what this mountain walk offers. The guidebook, prepared by David Laing and reviewed by Steve Faccio on staff at the Vermont Institute of Natural Science, is by far the most complete guide for use by the public that we have seen. Using it as you walk here is the next best thing to a course of studies in environmental science. Or, if you prefer, at the Hiking Center you can arrange to take a guided walk with a trained leader.

A short word about walking downhill: it sounds easier than it is. Walking uphill may challenge your aerobic system, but downhill challenges your feet, ankles, knees, and hips. If you are carrying a child or a heavy fannypack on your front, put them on your back. A walking stick is helpful going downhill for balance and to transfer weight to your arm (lead with your stick when going downhill). On steep terrain, plant your feet sideways to the slope. Like a skier, you can control your descent by traversing back and forth as you descend.

Wear good hiking boots with ground-gripping soles. A well-fitted hiking boot laced properly should hold the top of your foot and ankle in place, preventing your toes from mashing against the boot when you descend. Before descending, loosen your boots, pull up your socks snugly, and retie your boots firmly over the top of your foot to prevent injury to your toenails or toes. P.S. I learned this lesson the hard way and have a missing toenail to prove it.

The Spruce/Fir or Boreal Forest

The boreal forest is the largest in North America, stretching from Alaska across Canada to Labrador in a wide belt. It is found only in the most northern reaches of the United States and at high elevations, following the mountain ranges of Maine, New Hampshire, Vermont, and New York, and continuing southward down the high peaks of the Appalachians. It is composed primarily of **red spruce** and **balsam fir.** If you remember *fir is friendly and spruce is spiky* when you grasp a tree's

Balsam fir pinecones point upward on the branch.

branch, you'll be able to tell the two apart; spruce needles will prick your skin with their sharp, stiff points.

The conifers of the boreal forest are able to survive where few other plants or trees can. The soils are most often poor, because no nutrients are being added from outside sources and, in the cold temperatures, organic material decays very slowly. The canopy is solid and conifer needles create acidic soil conditions. The trees survive by remaining evergreen; this saves them the extra energy of putting out new leaves every year, and it provides them with year-round energy from the sun. At higher elevations, balsam fir is better adapted than spruce. By 3,700 feet, red spruce disappears. The extreme cover of the forest limits growth on the forest floor, but **mosses, goldthread,** and **wood sorrel** can be found. Other plants and grasses may be spotted along trails, because the trail itself provides an opening in the canopy where other, less shade tolerant plants can grow.

Mammals found in the spruce/fir forest are: **snowshoe hare, porcupine, red fox, red squirrel, chipmunk,** and **bobcat.** Many birds, primarily insect eaters, find excellent protection and nesting sites within the thick evergreen cover. Because of the cover, however, good sightings are difficult to come by. Learning to distinguish among the many warblers and other songbirds by their songs is a useful skill in this environment.

Getting There

Just west of Sherburne Center, turn south at the intersection of US 4 and Route 100 onto Killington Road. At its end is the Base Lodge, where the Merrell Hiking Center is located.

Affiliated Organizations

The Merrell Hiking Center at Killington Resort is open from 8:30 A.M. to 5:00 P.M. daily from mid-June to October, weather permitting. Early and late-season skiing can affect hiking, so call ahead first. Everyone using the trails must first sign a release.

In the Area

A stand of old-growth deciduous trees can be seen at Gifford Woods (page 188), a short distance north on Route 100.

Echo Lake Vista Trail
Camp Plymouth State Park

- **1.5 miles (0.8-mile round-trip to vista), 340-foot climb and descent**
- **1.75 hours (1 hour to vista and return)**
- **difficult**
- **wear hiking boots, and, if you like, bring a pan for gold**

The Echo Lake Vista Trail climbs to the top of a ridge and a view of the lake below. It then descends steeply to Buffalo Brook, of gold prospecting fame.

Cross Town Highway 42 at the park's entrance and follow the logging road 0.1 mile into the woods and turn left on the blue-blazed trail. A short walk brings you to another road. Turn left and climb to the cemetery. Across the cemetery, the trail continues to the vista. It is only 0.3 mile from the cemetery, but it climbs about 300 feet in that short distance, and the footing is difficult. At the vista, the valley opens below you, with Echo Lake to the south.

For those whose destination is only the vista, return on the same path. On your way back, you may want to spend a little time at the cemetery examining gravestones, some of which are beautifully carved in **slate** (see Slate History, page 173). To complete the loop,

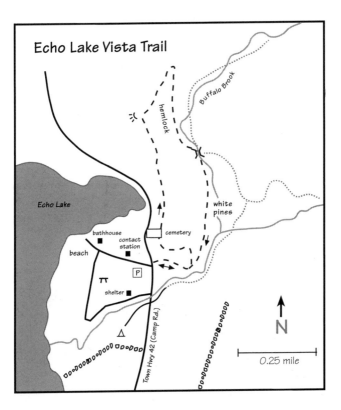

Echo Lake Vista Trail

hemlock

Buffalo Brook

Echo Lake

white
pines

bathhouse
contact
station
cemetery

beach

P

shelter

N

0.25 mile

Town Hwy 42 (Camp Rd.)

however, be advised that after a heavy rain or freezing
temperatures, you may have difficulty crossing Buffalo
Brook. The path to the brook drops as far as you just
climbed, so turning around at the brook and climbing
back up the ridge (the only way out) can be discourag-
ing. With that said, from the vista, follow the blue-
blazed trail down the ridge.

The trail zigzags steeply downhill among boulders and ledge. Patti stayed back to read gravestones, but I love trails where the terrain dictates their course. This one sometimes strays uphill to avoid large boulders, while at other times it passes through rock-formed crevices. At last, muted by hemlock boughs, I heard the sound of the brook below, and after a final switchback I descended to the shore of the brook.

The brook must be crossed on stepping stones, but they are randomly placed and not flat. When I was here, the water was just high enough that I would have had to jump from stone to stone, requiring delicate, one-foot balancing. I took the wiser course and removed my boots and socks and waded across. I then dried my blue feet and put my boots back on. After crossing the brook,

The old cemetery sits on a knoll above Echo Lake.

Echo Lake as seen from the vista.

the trail follows a dirt road. During **Vermont's gold rush,** prospectors poured up this road, staking their claims. People still **pan for gold** here (see next page). Although I didn't walk it, the road up the brook leads to the remains of mining operations. To explore them, check first with the park ranger for directions.

To return, turn right and follow the dirt road across the bridge and continue along the valley's floor (perhaps better characterized as a ravine). Very tall **white pine** grow along the brook. Through their towering crowns I could see that direct sunlight falls here only at midday. The taller a tree grows here, the longer it is in sunlight each day...and the taller it grows. Many old logging roads meander through this area and, if you go off the blue-blazed trail, finding your way can be quite confusing. The road eventually comes to a fork. Stay left and you will exit the logging road across from the campground where the trail began.

Gold in Them Thar Hills!

Well, sort of. It began when a young man, fresh back to Vermont from the California gold rush, was fishing in Buffalo Brook. He caught sight of a glitter—which he had the experience to recognize—and began panning. When word of his find got out, the rush was on. By 1855, the brook was known as **Gold Brook,** and a frenzy of prospectors descended upon it. At nearby Ply-

The last rays of the afternoon sun catch the tips of the tall pines growing from the deep valley of Bufffalo Brook.

mouth Five-Corners, a mill and crusher were erected. The prospecting continued for about 30 years. The fever subsided eventually as prospectors finally came to realize what George H. Perkins—state geologist from 1898 to 1933—had always felt: "It is entirely useless to throw away money, time, and labor seeking gold in Vermont."

According to Nicholas Ratcliff, who is updating the geologic map of Vermont for the U.S. Geological Survey, what little gold there is in Vermont came from the **Ottauquechee formation.** Located about 1.5 miles up Buffalo Brook, it has the **organic material** (carbonaceous sulfite schist) in the presence of **metal-bearing rocks** (serpentinites) that creates conditions for the formation of gold deposits.

Small amounts of gold-bearing quartz have been found, but most gold is **placer gold**—tiny particles washed out of glacial alluvia. It is mined on a small scale by panning, and amateur prospectors continue to pan for gold along Buffalo Brook and occasionally find tiny flakes. No permit is required for panning on state land.

Getting There

Camp Plymouth State Park is located north of Ludlow on Echo Lake. From Route 100, turn east in Tyson on Kingdom Road. In about 0.25 mile, take the first left onto Town Highway 42 (Camp Road). In another 0.25 mile, the park entrance is on the left.

Affiliated Organizations

Vermont Agency of Natural Resources, Department of Forests, Parks and Recreation (North Springfield office).

Springfield Area

Stewardship Nature Trail
The Vermont Country Store, Rockingham

- **less than a 1-mile loop, with shorter options; very mild slopes**
- **30 minutes**
- **easy**

A beautifully constructed trail with an informative printed guide explaining woodlot and wildlife habitat management practices.

The Vermont Country Store (VCS) in Rockingham is a popular stop for Vermonters and visitors alike. With the assistance of the Vermont Department of Forests and Parks and private consulting foresters, VCS is practicing forest stewardship and constructed this trail as part of the Vermont Forest Stewardship Program. **Stewardship** means managing land to optimize its use and productivity. VCS is managing its 80 acres for forest, wildlife, recreational, and aesthetic benefits. The Stewardship Nature Trail is a demonstration of specific practices that promote these land uses.

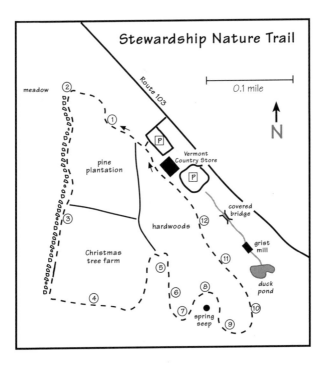

An entranceway and information board mark the trail's beginning just behind and to the right of the store. The trail guides available there—written by the husband-wife forester team of Don and Nina Huffer— explain the practices being implemented at each stop. The trail first enters a plantation of **red pine,** and we walked down its cathedrallike aisle, at the end of which is Stop 1. There, **tree thinning** to promote faster growth has been performed in one section of the red pine stand, but not in the other. The thinned trees receive more sunlight and grow faster (see page 191). The annual rings in tree cross-sections there show comparative growth rates between a **suppressed** and **dominant tree** of the same age. This thinning took place in 1993, and the differences in growth between the two stands should increase each year.

We continued into a large field where wetlands, a pond, and **primary forest succession** can be observed. Primary succession refers to the first species to move into abandoned pasture or farm land, or where forests

The Vermont Country Store Stewardship Nature Trail begins through a stand of carefully pruned red pine.

have been disturbed from the outside by fire, heavy cutting, blowdown, or other events.

From Stop 2, we turned back along a stone wall where **old sugar maples** were growing. One has a 20-foot branch that begins only four and a half feet off the ground and stretches far out over the trail—the lowest branch I've ever seen on such an old sugar maple. The tree must have begun life after the field was cleared. The ground would have been higher 150 years ago, so a low branch would have interfered with plowing the field. I imagine the original farmer trimmed off all the low branches in these fencerow trees, but decided to leave this one so his children could climb it. Each year he must have guided his team of horses out around the branch as he plowed. Perhaps he also used its shade to sit in as he ate his lunch.

The next stop is a high view upon a **balsam fir** Christmas tree farm. Stay on the trail here, because **poison ivy** is sharing the field with the Christmas trees. Remember: *Leaves of three, let it be.* The trail turns downhill at the end of the field and passes a large **bitternut hickory** tree that is heavily infested with **galls** created by a fungus rather than insects (see Montshire, page 320). The next two stops provide excellent examples of **forest-edge habitat** and a young **woodland thicket.**

A browsed juniper leaves a clue to what ate it. Look closely at its truncated twig ends: if they were bitten cleanly off, as if sliced with a knife, then a **snowshoe hare** fed there. By contrast, if they are ragged, then **whitetail deer** seized the twig between their molars and ripped it off. The height of the browsing indicates how high the snow was the previous winter.

The trail continues past clumps of **witch-hazel,** an oddity among trees. Rather than spring, it blooms in the late fall after losing its leaves. Then its ripened seeds that formed the year before are ejected with a loud *pop!* — shooting as far as 25 to 30 feet. A **vernal pool** lies to the right of the trail (see below). Next we came to an area where thinning was done to release old apple trees from crowding. They provide important **mast** (food) for deer and other animals. The apple tree nearest the trail at Stop 9 looks as if it had been blasted all around by a shotgun. The small holes, arranged in orderly horizontal rings around the tree, were made by **yellow-bellied sapsuckers,** a member of the woodpecker family. They make the holes and later return for the sap and insects attracted to it. Only one apple tree has holes. Such trees are called **sweet trees** and should be left when thinning trees. The sapsuckers will return to that one tree and leave the others alone.

At Stop 11, trees are variously marked, and the trail guide discusses the many — often conflicting — options a woodlot manager faces when thinning. Different objectives include: the species mix, the future rate of growth of residual trees, revenue generated by the cutting, wildlife habitat, and leaving healthy trees to reseed the forest. From Stop 12, a mixed hardwood forest, we returned to the store (noticing the huge, unusual **European white poplar** — an ornamental — along its east side).

A walk on this trail shows the many advantageous ways even a small plot of land can be managed for multiple purposes. In addition to providing habitat and commercial trees, Vermont Country Store invites people

An old "sweet" apple tree has been thoroughly perforated in horizontal rows by yellow-bellied sapsuckers.

to cross country ski here in the winter, providing yet another use—recreation.

Vernal Pools

There is a **vernal pool** (or **spring seep**) at Stop 8. This is a low depression that fills with water during the spring runoff but dries up as the summer gets hotter. Until recently, such areas were not given much attention (unless to fill them in), but biologists now have determined that they provide a very important habitat for

A vernal pool or spring seep, dry by summer, provides invaluable habitat in the spring for many amphibians.

amphibians, such as **peepers, wood frogs,** and **spotted salamanders.** Here they mate and lay eggs in the spring, while such predators as **herons** and **kingfishers** are watching for a meal at ponds and lakes, not really aware of the vernal pools because of their ephemeral nature.

If you want to witness the rather unusual sight of hundreds or thousands of these creatures performing their instinctive spring rituals together in these small woodland pools, you've got to watch April's weather carefully. After each spring rain, check the temperature. The night after a rain when the temperature will be near or above 42°F will be the one night they all migrate. Grab your flashlight, put on your rubber boots, and head for a vernal pool. The show will be well worth the trouble, and, with no admission, you can take the entire family.

Another creature that makes use of vernal pools is the **fairy shrimp.** This one-inch crustacean loves the backstroke: while swimming on its back, it uses its tail to wash algae and small organisms up to its mouth. It has adapted to vernal pools by laying eggs that can lie dormant for up to 20 years, surviving lengthy droughts.

Getting There

Take Exit 6 off I-91 toward Rockingham and go west on Route 103. In about 2 miles, the Vermont Country Store will be on your left. The entrance to the Nature Trail is to the right of the store behind it.

Affiliated Organizations

The Vermont Country Store. (For Vermonters interested in more information on the Vermont Forest Steward-ship Program, contact your county forester or the Vermont Agency of Natural Resources, Office of Information, Department of Forests, Parks and Recreation.)

In the Area

A path to the left of VCS goes through a small **covered bridge** and on to an old **gristmill** with a working water wheel. Just beyond the mill is a lovely small **duck pond.**

Bryant Farm Nature Trail
Meeting Waters YMCA Camp, Springfield

- **0.5 mile**
- **30 minutes**
- **easy**

A walk to the banks of the Black River offering a variety of wildflowers, plants, trees, and birds — including bamboolike Japanese knotweed.

Bryant Farm Nature Trail is located right next to I-91 and does not offer the quiet of the countryside. This small pocket of nature-rich land on the riverbank contrasts with the urgency of all the cars and trucks flying by on the interstate above. It is, however, a place to appreciate the complexity and tenacity with which nature is holding her own here at the road's side and river's edge. It makes me realize how little of the world I see cruising through it at 65 MPH.

In 1870, Sam Brown built a large, beautiful farmhouse along US 5 and, like a preponderance of Vermonters at the time, raised sheep. The flat area on which you park is one of the many fertile terraces left by glacial Lake Hitchcock (see page 66). The William J. Bryants purchased the farm in the early 1920s. It then consisted of 120 acres of forest, field, and riverfront. In addition to

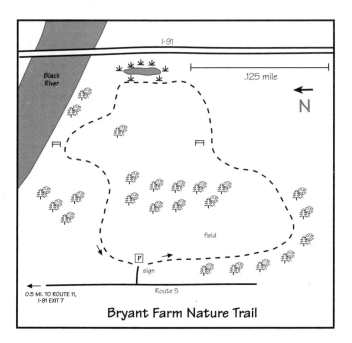

Bryant Farm Nature Trail

Black River

I-91

.125 mile

N

field

P

sign

Route 5

0.5 MI. TO ROUTE 11,
I-91 EXIT 7

livestock, the Bryants were well known for their **Morgan horses,** Vermont's state animal.

Life along US 5 changed drastically when I-91 was built in the 1960s, and like many farms in the area, the Bryant farm was sold. In 1986, Meeting Waters YMCA in Bellows Falls purchased 39 acres to be used as a regional summer day camp for area children. In 1988, they purchased an additional 13 acres. The camp pavilion is located on the upper field, across US 5 from the nature walk.

Bryant Farm is on the Black River, which meets the Connecticut River just beyond the I-91 bridge in the background.

A map of the walk's route is engraved on a large, handsome wooden sign near the parking area. The sign and numbered posts along the trail, along with a written guide, were an Eagle Scout project by Jeremy Davis of Springfield.

To the right of the parking area, **pioneer species** are reclaiming the cleared land. **Sumac, raspberry, blackberry,** and **strawberry** plants can be found, as well as **mullein,** whose large, soft pastel-green leaves are very fuzzy (leading to its common name of **velvet-leaf**). The hairs on its leaves reflect the sunlight, protecting it from overdrying.

At the edge of the forest is a large **black oak** tree. Oak trees have the confusing habit of freely hybridizing in the wild, making it difficult to distinguish among them—especially between red and black oak. Black oak leaves have fine white hairs along their stems on the underside and its inner bark is bright orange. **Wild grape vine** (see page 167) has invaded many of the trees in this area.

A grove of **quaking aspen** covers the bank as you descend. Examine a leaf's stem closely and you will see how it is flattened where it joins the leaf. This is why aspen leaves flutter, even in barely moving air. At the foot of the bank is a grassy area. **Grasses**—whose seeds are grain—are as important to wildlife as they are to us (see page 148). When settlers first arrived, Vermont was almost completely forested. Without sunlight, there is no grass, and with no grass, their was no feed for their animals. It was important to clear land quickly. In a pinch, they **girdled** trees by cutting through the bark and cambium all the way around the trunk. That killed the tree, letting the sunlight hit the ground through its dead branches.

The next section of trail offers visitors a variety of flowers, ground cover, trees, and wildlife habitat. **Ash-leaf maples** (commonly called **box-elder,** though it is a maple) produce seeds that are a favorite of beautiful yellow **evening grosbeaks.** Many old-pasture species of flowers (weeds to a farmer) grow here, including **yarrow, purple vetch, spirea,** and **goldenrod.** Authorities claim that you can't be allergic to goldenrod, or any flower that has a colored bloom. Colored blooms mean the plant is pollinated by insects and thus doesn't broadcast its pollen. Since its bloom does not attract insects, **ragweed** does broadcast pollen—and is the likely culprit in allergic reactions.

In the middle of the field is a stand of what looks like bamboo, but is, in fact, **Japanese knotweed.** It spreads vigorously by root sprouting and soon invades all available space. Its dead stalks protect the young shoots in the springtime. **Grouse, quail, mourning doves, pheasant, deer,** and **woodcock** all enjoy its shoots and seeds.

We passed a stand of **staghorn sumac** (see below) and came to a bench by the river. It was occupied by Auld Angus Black from Peru, Vermont, whose business card reads "birdwatcher and fisherman (fly, spin, worm)." No fish, however, were seen lying about.

Wander the riverbank as the Black River flows by and you may find **motherwort, jewelweed, spotted Joe-Pye-weed, blue-eyed grass, bird's-foot trefoil, asters, Queen Anne's lace,** and **red clover** (the Vermont state flower). Among the trees are **hackberry, American elm,** and **cottonwood.** The branches of **silver maple** and **black willow** can be found hanging out over the river. Auld Angus isn't the only one who fishes here. **Blue herons** do as well (probably more successfully). According to Jeremy's notes, original settlers chose this site because of easy access to the Black River and Fort #4 was just across the Connecticut River.

A gravel path brought us back to the parking lot. Although Bryant Farm is in a setting quite different from most nature walks, the lush river bottomland here is full of surprises. I always find places like this a good antidote to an overromanticized, "Ansel Adams" view of nature. We tend to find beauty only when everything is composed according to our own aesthetic rules. Here, nature has been allowed to follow her own rule: chaotic, free-for-all life in every niche available.

Staghorn Sumac

Staghorn sumac is a pioneer species likely recognized by everyone. When grown in the open, it spreads underground, putting up new sprouts all around it and developing into stands of pure sumac, such as that seen at Bryant Farm. Driving on I-91, you can see many such stands in the median strip. If you look at each stand of trees as a whole—like the single large plant that it is— you will see it has a characteristic shape. The tallest

The typical shape of a stand of sumac sharing the same root system.

(and oldest) trees are always in the middle of the stand, while the trees around it get progressively shorter. Their tops form a beautiful curving shape, especially noticeable in the winter, when clusters of red berries top the bare, branching spikes.

The berries are rich in vitamin A, though not a preferred food of animals or birds. When you see birds at the fruit in the winter, it is more likely they are after the insects and spiders who have hunkered down within the berry clusters. The fruits can also be used to make a tart summer drink, giving sumac its traditional nickname, **lemonade tree.**

Getting There

Bryant Farm Nature Trail is on US 5, just south of Springfield. From the junction of US 5 and Route 11, go 0.3 mile south on US 5. The sign for Bryant Farm Nature Trail is on your left.

Affiliated Organizations

Meeting Waters YMCA, Bellows Falls.

In the Area

Two walks we highly recommend are not far from Bryant Farm: North Springfield Bog (see next page) and Springweather Nature Area (page 232).

North Springfield Bog
North Springfield

- a very short walk to and through the bog
- 30 minutes
- very easy
- bring wildflower book and magnifying glass

Charles Johnson, Vermont state naturalist, said this small bog has some of the finest examples of bog plants in the state, including an abundance of unusually large carnivorous pitcher-plants.

Stroll up the dirt road several hundred yards to a timber barricade. The bog entrance is on your right. Before starting into the bog, observe its setting; it lies in the bottom of a bowl (kettle) formed by the surrounding land. This is a true **boreal kettle bog** (see below), because the species found here are typically found farther north in colder climates. Strictly speaking, a **bog**—as opposed to a **fen**—is a depression whose only supply of water comes from rain and runoff. A true bog—like this one—has no inlet or outlet. As a result, very few nutrients find their way into it.

It is also a **quaking bog,** since its thick mat of organic matter actually floats on water far below. Although the mat is more than 40 feet thick, it has not

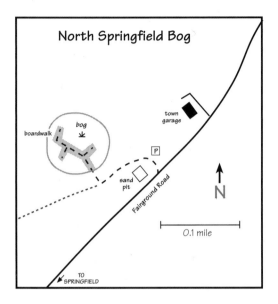

North Springfield Bog

yet reached the bottom of the kettle. This mat has accu-
mulated over a period of about 10,000 years, and as new
organic material is added, it compresses the matter
below it, growing thicker from the top. Walking unaid-
ed in quaking bogs is tricky business. People need to be
protected from sinking into the bog, while delicate bog
plants need protection from people trampling them.
The walkways that make it easily accessible were constructed as a mutual project by the **Ascutney Mountain
Audubon Society** and federal and state governments.
The decision to use synthetic materials obviated the
need for driving pilings or using chemically treated
wood, avoiding any damage to the bog. As you pass

over the boardwalk it soon becomes apparent that it, too, is floating.

A bog's most important denizen is **sphagnum moss.** A hundred centuries ago, a sphagnum mat began here on branches and debris that had fallen in the water. Sphagnum moss has made a special adaptation to survive in a bog's waters. Most mosses are **vascular;** that is, they have roots that absorb nutrients and transport them throughout the plant. Carbohydrates from photosynthesis are also transported from the leaves to the roots. Sphagnum moss, however, has no vascular system. Instead, it directly absorbs tremendous

A floating boardwalk runs through the small boreal kettle bog in North Springfield.

amounts of water to obtain the scant nutrients available in a bog. Because of its tremendous absorption capability—up to 20 times its own weight in water—sphagnum was used as diapers by Native Americans, and is again being used for superabsorbent products. It is also acidic, which makes it antiseptic, and was used from the Middle Ages until World War I to dress wounds.

Sphagnum competes by actively poisoning the bog; as it breaks down, it gives off **humic acid,** creating an inhospitable environment for all but the most specialized plants. When it dies, new masses of growth continue to build on top of it. Because there is so little oxygen in a bog's water, decay is almost completely retarded. It is in such bogs that ancient organic artifacts, like viking ships, are sometimes found intact. Over centuries, dead sphagnum and organic material that falls into the bog pile up, compressing the layers below. This compressed material, sometimes 60 feet deep or more, is mined and sold as common **peat moss** for garden use.

That makes a bog a biological laboratory—or perhaps *museum* is a better word. Each year, the pollens, leaves, and other debris that it collects are covered by new layers of peat. The buried peat preserves a chronological record of plant life in that area over thousands of years. Researchers can then take a core of peat and analyze its contents downward to obtain an understanding of the natural history of the area through time.

For example, by noting the changing mix of species over thousands of years, they can perceive long-term weather trends. From such studies, scientists have learned that between 5,000 and 3,000 years ago, plants that required a warm climate were growing in Vermont.

This period is called the **climatic optimum.** The analysis of the peat then shows the pollens of these plants disappeared and those of plants adapted to colder climates reappeared. A few relics of the warmer times still remain—the black gum trees in the Black Gum Swamp and oak/hickory forests in the Glen Lake area.

The North Springfield Bog is known for its abundance of unusually large leafed **pitcher-plants.** These unmistakable plants are found along the boardwalk and throughout the bog. Their heavily veined red leaf, appearing early in the spring, is shaped and sealed like a water pitcher and holds a pool of water within. They generate an odor that attracts insects, but when one

Three young pitcher-plants. Not only do they entice, trap, drown, and digest insects, but the larvae of some insects make a home in them, while spiders may spin a web across the mouth of the pitcher to steal the insects attracted by the plant's scent.

lands on the lip of the plant, it finds it slippery and falls in. Although it struggles upward to escape, tiny down-pointing hairs prevent it from climbing back out. When it succumbs and falls into the water at the bottom, the pitcher-plant secretes enzymes that dissolve and digest the insect. It is thus able to absorb its daily recommended dose of nitrogen, otherwise unavailable in the bog.

The pitcher-plant puts out a two-foot bloom in late June that has a fascinating construction. Bees enter it, picking up pollen, but must leave by a different route that makes it impossible for them to pollinate the same plant. This ensures cross-pollination.

The bloom of the pitcher-plant may be as high as two feet and forms on a separate stem.

What may look like tussocks of solid ground in the bog are masses of peat and sphagnum mixed with the remains of other plants. On the far side of the bog opposite the entrance, some small evergreens are establishing themselves on a hummock; these are **black spruces.** They develop a widely spreading mass of roots so they can grow upright in the peat and still resist the wind. A nonscientific but reliable way to distinguish between red and black spruce is its location: if the location is dry, it is a **red spruce;** if it is wet, it is a **black spruce.**

Varieties of **blueberry** and **cranberry**—both lovers of acidic environments—can be seen growing throughout. Blueberries are bushes, but the delicate cranberry creeps along the ground. The cranberry's pink bloom in the late spring has a curled-back cap with what looks like a beak pointing out. Its name derives from its flower's resemblance to a crane.

In warm months, you can see the world's smallest flowering plant—**duckweed**—floating on top of pools of water. Look for tiny little green disks, about the size of a match head. A tiny root dangles into the water from each one. Duckweed are capable of flowering, but they most often reproduce by budding and can almost completely cover areas of stagnant water. Ingenious little plants, they produce an excess of starch late in the summer. That makes them heavier and they sink to the bottom before ice forms. They use up the starch over the winter and by spring, are lighter again and bob back to the surface after the ice melts.

As you explore the North Springfield Bog from its walkways, be thankful for the efforts of the many individuals who saw to its preservation and made it easily accessible.

How Did This Boreal Kettle Bog Form?

As the last glacier flowed over Vermont, a large chunk of ice broke off and was buried in poorly draining **glacial till** — the sand, gravel, clay, and rocks carried (or pushed) by the glacier. When the glacier melted away more than 10,000 years go, this chunk of ice finally melted, leaving its depression — called a **kettle** — filled with water. The deep water in the depression created a cooler environment than surrounding areas. Even on a warm summer's day, you will find that a bog's water is surprisingly cool. Its temperature inhibits plants from absorbing water through their roots and helps retard decay.

The decay of organic matter in the kettle early in its life exhausted the water's oxygen. Because there was no continual supply of fresh water, the oxygen was not replenished. Plants that may have first established themselves here died off as nutrients and oxygen disappeared. Sphagnum moss moved in and began acidifying the water and building up a floating peat mass. Today, after 10,000 years of bog-building activity, the peat supports the highly specialized plants that have come to depend on the unique environment of the bog.

Getting There

The North Springfield Bog is near the Town Garage on Fairground Road. From Route 106, take Route 11 west from Springfield. Take the first right onto Fairground Road. In 2.0 miles, the Town Garage facility is ahead on the left. Before the garage, turn left next to the sand pit and park. The bog is several hundred yards up the dirt road to the left that is blocked from vehicles by rubble.

Affiliated Organizations

The North Springfield Bog is on Springfield town property. The Ascutney Mountain Audubon Society, aided by junior high school students and partially funded by a Land and Water Conservation grant, opened this bog for study by installing the synthetic floating boardwalk that provides access.

Springweather Nature Area
North Springfield Lake

- **choose the length of your walk**
- **easy**
- **bring binoculars and a bird identification book**

This area provides a rich experience of nature, including exceptional bird-watching: 160 species, 20 of them warblers, have been sighted, and many uncommon birds nest here.

In 1978, Eleanor Ellis had an idea: to develop a trail system for bird-watchers and nature lovers on U.S. Army Corps of Engineers land at North Springfield Lake. The Springweather Nature Area is the fruit of that vision and the first cooperative effort between the Corps and the Audubon Society. The trails meander through 70 acres that the society leases for a nominal sum.

The Red Trail (about 30 minutes)

We met Eleanor—who graciously offered to walk the trails with us—one early spring morning. She led us to the bulletin board at the junction of the Red and Blue trails, where a stand of nodding trillium grows. All four species found in Vermont—**nodding, red, painted,** and **white trillium**—could be found in the park in years past, but no one has spotted the white trillium in the last few years.

Nearly two dozen species of **fern** grow in Spring-weather as well. Across the road are stands of **intermediate** and **marginal woodferns** and across the gully at the beginning of the Red Trail are **maidenhair ferns.** If you stay left at R3 (see map), you enter a series of short trails, collectively known as the **Fern Trail.** On these trails can be found more ferns, such as the **interrupted, ostrich** (see page 322), **crested,** and **sensitive.** (The trails are very clearly marked and inconspicuously blazed with small arrows, whose color matches that of the trail.) We walked the Red Trail through a stand of **Norway spruce,** where **ruffed grouse** are often found.

Down the side trail from R7 is **wild ginger,** and at the end of this spur is a bench from which the views and birds of the area may be enjoyed. We passed another bench on the Red Trail and reached the start of the Green Trail at R9. To shorten the walk, continue on the Red Trail loop. It follows a field in the process of succession, with large **anthills, spirea,** and **shade-intolerant trees.** When it reaches the gravel road, turn right to the parking area.

The Green Trail (an additional hour, including return)

The Green Trail continues to an area of open grass overlooking the valley below, with views to **Mt. Ascutney** (see page 238). At times of high water, you may be seeing North Springfield Lake rather than the valley floor. This is a great vantage point from which to observe waterfowl. **Wood ducks, mallards, blacks,** and **mergansers** nest here, and during migration, **green-winged teals** and many other species pass through. **Great blue**

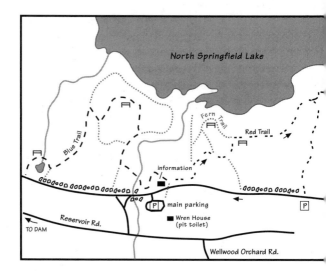

herons are often seen in the marsh. On a previous walk here, Eleanor and a friend had watched two **moose** wading below in the water as they grazed on the aquatic plants.

At the next lookout and bench, 100 feet above the valley, Eleanor told us of canoeing to this bench during the **June 1984 flood,** when the reservoir was full. It was hard to imagine the enormous volume of water it had taken to turn the deep valley into a lake and raise the level to where we were standing. A similar flood occurred again in April 1987.

The trail turned east to a spot at the top of a ridge where we were looking directly into the tops of the oak trees growing in the ravine below — a perfect spot from

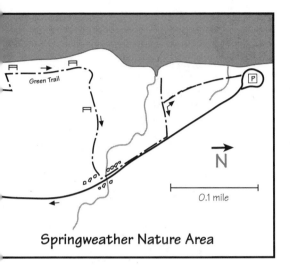

Springweather Nature Area

which to observe birds that prefer high perches, like **scarlet tanagers.** In the upland areas of Springweather are **American woodcock, kestrel, wood thrush, veery, black-and-white warblers, black-throated green warblers,** and many others.

Reaching the gravel road, Eleanor led us north to its end. It passes through a wonderful **ecotone** — the transition between forest and open areas — that is a prime bird-feeding area. **Chestnut-sided warblers** and the **common yellowthroat** are seen here, and in some years, **blue-gray gnatcatchers** (which, with their long upright tails, look like miniature mockingbirds). **Least flycatchers** can also be spotted in the shrubs at the edge of the marsh. From here, we walked slowly back on the pic-

North Springfield Lake from the Green Trail. As part of the flood control system, the reservoir is kept relatively empty. During the flood of 1984, the water would have been at my feet from where this photo was taken.

turesque road, overhung with trees and bordered with **alder, mountain ash, pussy willow,** and other shrubs.

The Blue Trail (0.75 hour)

We went left this time at the bulletin board on the Blue Trail. The first short stretch of this trail is an exceptionally pretty little walk, with its narrow pathway weaving among the trees. **White pine, ironwood,** and **bigtooth aspen** grow here. We crossed a brook on a footbridge and climbed to the field, where several trails provide options. In a grove of cottonwoods at B8 is a small pond or **vernal pool** that may be dry in the summer (see page 213). With stepping-stones over the creek and another bench, it is an idyllic spot that schoolchildren often visit to learn about pond ecology. In the field north of it is the **demonstration project;** the Ascutney Mountain Audubon Society and Springfield Garden Club are developing this area by adding flowers and shrubs that attract birds and wildlife. The project demonstrates ways anyone can bring more birds and wildlife to their backyards.

Tucked away into the Springweather Nature Area are two new **osprey nesting platforms.** They were not yet occupied when we were there. Keep an eye out for the platforms standing tall in the marshy valley at a distance and determine if osprey have begun nesting on them. With that, we concluded our walk, much

Eleanor Ellis, whose vision and hard work resulted in the creation of Springweather, strolls with Patti Mikolas down the access road that links the trails.

impressed with what Eleanor and scores of society members and the enthusiastic cooperation of the Corps have accomplished. They set out to create a place "to contemplate the mysteries of nature, to observe the changing seasons, to open your senses to the beauty of the world around you." They succeeded—and we hope you get a chance to visit this special area.

Mt. Ascutney

Mt. Ascutney's core was formed of molten rock that forced itself upward into overlying schists. This happened twice, though neither molten intrusion broke the surface. The magma slowly cooled into a **pluton,** a domelike plug beneath the surface, similar to that which formed Black Mountain (page 68). The first **intrusion** was syenite magma, similar to granite but containing less quartz. The second was granite magma. Through the millennia, erosion and glaciation carried away the softer rock of the peneplain surrounding Mt. Ascutney, leaving the more resistant **syenite** and **granite.**

Mt. Ascutney's formation was part of the process that created the White Mountains—making it the only Vermont mountain associated with the high peaks of New Hampshire. At 120 million years old, it is also **Vermont's youngest mountain,** three to four times younger than the bedrock around it. Rising 2,250 feet from the floor of the Connecticut River Valley to an elevation of 3,144 feet, Mt. Ascutney stands high above everything else and is thus an excellent example of a **monadnock.**

When glaciers scoured its surface, they left north-south **striations** in the rock, visible at its summit. They

Mt. Ascutney rises alone above the Connecticut River Valley to stand sentinel.

also plucked rocks off its southern side and carried them along. When the glacier melted, the rocks, known as **erratics,** were dropped randomly along the glacier's course all the way to Massachusetts in what is called the **Ascutney Boulder Train.** The Dumplings on the trail to Hamilton Falls (page 94) are well-known erratics.

If you enjoy hiking, any of Ascutney's four main summit trails make for a good day. My favorite is the Weathersfield Trail. It passes 84-foot **Crystal Cascade,** where evidence of a rare formation called a **ring dike**— the rough circle around the mountain where the magma oozed up to form its core—can be seen. Fragments of rock that the magma failed to melt are visible above the falls. The Ascutney Trails Association offers an excellent trail guide and map of the mountain. For those who are not up to hiking, an access road off Route 44A leads to its eastern face near the summit, where trails lead to many vantage points to enjoy the views, watch birds, or watch people jump off the summit to hang-glide.

Getting There

The Springweather Nature Area is on the east side of North Springfield Lake. From its intersection with Route 143 in Springfield, take Route 106 north. At 2.5 miles, turn right on Reservoir Road. Pass the dam and Recreation Area entrance on the left and take the next turn left into the Springweather Nature Area. Park to the right. The bulletin board is across the road. A pit toilet shaped like a wren house is just above the parking lot.

Affiliated Organizations

The Springweather Nature Area is on U.S. Army Corps of Engineers land. It is managed by the Ascutney Mountain Audubon Society.

In the Area

Both the Pine Hill Trail (next page) and Lower Village Nature Trail (page 247), are in North Springfield Lake Recreation Area. In addition, there are opportunities for biking, horseback riding, canoeing, swimming, boating, fishing, and hunting. In the winter, trails may be used for cross country skiing, snowshoeing, and dogsledding, and many snowmobile trails pass through the area. Drive out on the dam for a spectacular view of North Springfield Lake with Mt. Ascutney rising behind it.

Pine Hill Trail
Stoughton Pond

- **0.5 mile**
- **45 minutes**
- **easy, some minor uphill walking**

This trail presents interesting natural features and views of the small lake formed by the Stoughton Pond dam, part of the North Springfield Lake reservoir system.

The trail starts at the paved path from the parking lot to the beach. At Station 1 is a **butternut tree,** sometimes known as the **white walnut** (see page 244). From here, we watched several pair of **common mergansers** diving in the pond. At Station 3 are **paper** and **yellow birches.** The inner bark of birches can be eaten raw, dried and ground for flour, or boiled like noodles. The sap of both trees can be tapped and boiled down into a syrup about half as sweet as maple syrup. Station 4 is a bench set among the birches with a view of the pond.

The trail continues along the shore to a wet area. Salamanders and frogs depend upon such **vernal pools** for mating (see page 213). At Stations 5 and 6 are a colony of ferns on the right and wild grasses along the shore. **Grasses** are important to wildlife for protection and nesting materials. They also provide food for **deer, wild turkeys,** and **rabbits. Grass seeds** also have the

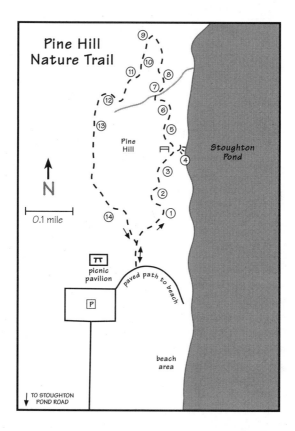

Pine Hill
Nature Trail

Stoughton
Pond

Pine
Hill

N

0.1 mile

picnic
pavilion

P

paved path to beach

beach
area

TO STOUGHTON
POND ROAD

unusual ability to stay dormant until conditions are right for growth (see page 148).

The path then crosses a small bridge over a gully. Station 8 is uphill along the gully. The hard wood and muscular-looking bark of the trees here account for their popular name of **ironwood** or **musclewood.** At its

*The Pine Hill Trail
follows the lakeshore,
passing a wolf pine.*

north (windward) end, the pond is marshy, and the mergansers had headed for the protection of the aquatic plants. The trail turns and climbs uphill to Station 9, the logging road used by the Stoughton family for many years. It now provides a pleasant walk through a hemlock forest.

At Station 12, **clubmoss** blankets the forest floor where there is acidic, damp soil. Clubmosses have changed a lot in 300 million years; they used to grow as large as the pine trees are today. We continued steeply uphill to a wide snowmobile trail, which we followed back to the picnic area. Look for **elm** trees on your way back. Their double-toothed leaves feel sandpapery and one side of the leaf joins the stem below the other side, similar to **witch-hazel.**

Butternut Trees

Alas, Vermont is just north of the range of the stately **black walnut** tree (with a few individual exceptions), but the **butternut** is found in Vermont's more poorly drained areas and bottomlands. Both trees are highly regarded for their wood and their large, edible, rich nuts. Native Americans boiled butternuts and hardened the oil that floated to the surface into a fatty substance they used like butter—hence its name. **Black bear, wild turkey,** and **whitetail deer** eat the nuts to help add an extra layer of fat for the winter, while squirrels race against them to bury as many as they can. The tree most often reseeds from the occasional nut a squirrel forgets to recover by spring.

As with black walnut, the casing around the nut is difficult to get off and will stain your hands brown for weeks to come. Not surprisingly, the husks were used by settlers to make an orange-brown fabric dye. To crack and eat butternuts, the best way I know to remove the casings is to spread the nuts on the driveway and drive your car back and forth over them, but eat the nuts quickly, for they go rancid rapidly. It's against the law now, but Native Americans also crushed the hulls of butternuts and shagbark hickory nuts and used them to poison and harvest fish.

The distinctive leaf scar of a butternut tree, with its three bundle scars, looks like the face of a monkey.

Butternut wood is prized for how easily it is worked and for the satiny finish it takes, which mellows with age. Butternut veneer was used to panel stately and dignified rooms, and many a church altar was built of it. However, veneer-quality trees with tall, straight trunks have become extremely scarce. There is a local legend that a butternut "nut" once traveled from village to village distributing them, as Johnny did with apple seeds. As a result, many old homes in southern Vermont have a dooryard butternut spreading its powerful branches low to the ground—and a lot of fat and happy squirrels waiting each fall for its nuts to ripen (see Gordon Welchman, page 289).

As an aid in identification, it is the only common tree in Vermont that has **chambered pith.** If you slice a twig longitudinally, you will see that the pith is composed of membranes separated by spaces.

Getting There

Stoughton Pond is at the north end of North Springfield Lake. From Springweather Nature Area, go north on Reservoir Road, whose name changes to Stoughton Pond Road. (From the west side of the lake or Lower Village in Perkinsville, go north on Route 106 and take a right onto Stoughton Pond Road.) On Stoughton Pond Road, turn north into the park entrance.

Affiliated Organizations

U.S. Army Corps of Engineers, North Springfield Lake.

In the Area

See *In the Area* in Springweather Nature Area (page 240) for more information.

Lower Village Nature Trail
Perkinsville

- **0.75 mile**
- **45 minutes**
- **easy**

A beautiful stand of beech, a vast meadow, and a marsh attract many birds. A pleasant, wooded walk leads to views of Mt. Ascutney and possible sightings of whitetail deer.

The Lower Village was once just that: a small enclave of families and farmhouses, a cotton mill, power dam, covered bridge, cemetery, and slaughterhouse. These structures were either razed or relocated to provide a much-needed flood zone for the Black River. The U.S. Army Corps of Engineers is improving the parking and trailhead signage, so it will be more clearly marked than when we visited. In the open fields near the parking lot, **tree swallows** were nesting in **bluebird** boxes. To attract bluebirds, always put up two houses about 20 feet apart. Most species of birds will not nest close to others of their own species. Thus, a swallow will likely nest in one, but will leave the second free for less-aggressive bluebirds.

We were greeted with a wonderful symphony of sounds when we parked. Simultaneously we heard **doves** cooing, a **barred owl** hooting (*who cooks for you, who cooks for you all*), a **grouse** drumming, and in the distance, a **rooster** crowing. The trail leads into the

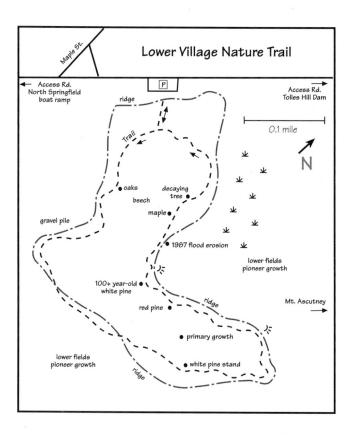

woods where it goes north along the ridge. Beech trees are growing abundantly in this rich soil. We curved around to the south and a vista. There we could see a marshy area below and fields beyond. Beyond that is the Stoughton Pond dam. In the distance, towering above everything, is Mt. Ascutney (page 238).

A tree swallow nesting in one of the houses provided by the U.S. Army Corps of Engineers awaits a meal.

From here and along the trail, you can scan the area below with binoculars for birds. Better yet, you can leave the trail at the second vantage point to walk the fields and edges of the marsh. There, **alder, pussy willow,** and **red-osier dogwood** create wonderful habitat for dozens of species of birds. The brush growing in the field show signs of heavy deer browsing, and in the fall, the deer frequently feed in the forest on **beechnuts.** In the morning or evening, you may spot them in the meadow.

From the second vantage point, the trail curves around to continue southwest through the woods and back to the parking lot.

Beech Trees

If I were writing this book at the dawn of history, I might have written it on beech bark. The earliest Sanskrit characters were scratched into sheets of its bark, and our word *book* is from the Anglo-Saxon *boc*, which means a letter or character. *Boc,* in turn, derived from *beece,* for the tree.

The bark of the beech is its most recognizable feature; it is smooth and gray, and since the days when colonists first settled North America, people seem to be irresistibly drawn to carve their initials into it. I saw a large beech in New Hampshire's Pisgah State Park carved with a set of initials and the date July 11, 1822. I always keep my eyes out for, and occasionally spot, what are known as **bear trees**—beech trees whose bark shows the claw marks of bears who climbed them to get at the sweet, oily beechnuts.

Bears are not alone in savoring beechnuts. They were a staple of Stone Age man and are still eaten by European peasants. To fatten hogs, farmers through history have driven them into beech forests to forage for nuts. In the wild, they are eagerly sought by **whitetail deer, ruffed grouse, wild turkey, pheasant, raccoon, fox, rabbit, porcupine, opossums,** and **red, gray,** and **flying squirrels.** Even **wood ducks** appear to do best in regions that contain nut-bearing trees, such as beeches, oaks, and hickories.

Beeches, as those at the Lower Village testify, are signs of good soil. They love the same conditions preferred by farmers: deep, level, dark loam on limestone. The beech is a successful competitor in many ways.

An American beech tree with bear claw marks in its bark. Bears savor beechnuts—as do most mammals.

Because it is extremely shade tolerant, it can—with its frequent mate, eastern hemlock—seed and grow in the understory of other less-tolerant, shorter-lived trees, which they will eventually overtop. Beech leaves are full of **tannin** and create acidic soils that drive out other non-acid-loving species.

But beech is not doing so well against **beech bark disease.** This disease began in Nova Scotia and has spread throughout the tree's range. The **nectria fungus** enters the tree through openings bored by **scale insects.** Once a tree is stricken, the fungus causes cankers in its bark and eventually kills it. However, beech can reproduce vegetatively by sending up sprouts from its stump and roots. As with **sumac, locust,** and **aspen,** root sprouting can result in a grove of **cloned trees,** all with the same genes.

Getting There

The Lower Village Nature Trail is located in Perkinsville, north of Springfield on Route 106. In Perkinsville, turn east from Route 106 onto Maple Street, which becomes the Recreation Area access road. Turn left at its end; parking is on the right.

Affiliated Organizations

U.S. Army Corps of Engineers, North Springfield Lake.

In the Area

See *In the Area* in Springweather Nature Area (page 240) for more information.

Wilgus Tree Identification Trail

Town of Weathersfield

- **0.5 mile**
- **30 minutes**
- **very easy**

The Springfield Boy Scouts developed this tree identification trail, where about a dozen species of trees and shrubs are identified. The riverbank walk is a quiet and easy stroll.

The trail starts at the southern end of the park, past the lean-tos. It proceeds along the river and then loops back higher on the bank. Many tree and shrub specimens are marked by carefully made wooden signs. The tree's common name, Latin name, and a brief description of its use or importance are posted. The park land was donated by Colonel and Mrs. William Wilgus. Colonel Wilgus, born in 1865, was an internationally famous civil engineer who specialized in structures relating to transportation. Among his many accomplishments was conceiving a centralized underground railroad terminal that led to the building of New York City's Grand Central Station.

The river here is narrow and straight. We walked it early one morning under a canopy of arching trees with rays of sunlight slanting through them. It was quiet,

except for a single **phoebe,** persistently calling *fee-be, fee-be.* Its two-note song resembles that of the **black-capped chickadee,** but is throatier and has more overtones, as though it really is trying to repeat its name. As we walked, I tried to imagine Grand Central Station at that same moment—an endless stream of hands sliding down the oaken banister as passengers, pressed front to back, rushed to catch the shuttle. Trying to picture the scene made it very easy to understand why Vermont is loved by so many people.

Early spring on the riverside Tree Identification Trail at Wilgus State Park.

If you'd like to enhance your walk here with a tree identification challenge, see if you can find the **hackberry tree** that Rick White—a forester with the Department of Forests, Parks and Recreation—spotted. Hackberry has coarsely toothed, heart-shaped leaves that are uneven at their base and dark, warty knobs on its bark.

Identifying Trees

Identifying trees is an art and a science. Picking a leaf and taking it home to consult a book does not always lead to a certain identification. Many trees, e.g., hornbeam, ironwood, the birches, elms, cherries, and plum trees, have leaves that take some careful, detailed observation to identify—and distinguishing between single

Ironwood's look of sinewy strength explains its old-time popular name of musclewood.

examples of some of them can be a muddle. Other trees, such as northern, black, scarlet, and pin oak, have over-lapping leaf-shape variations that can make a certain identification based on leaves alone impossible. To further confuse matters, some species freely hybridize and can stump experienced dendrologists. And, of course, in the winter, when many Vermonters are out selecting trees to cut for firewood, leaf shapes can't be used at all.

To identify a tree by its leaves, there are many qualities to observe beyond its shape. Are they single leaves or multiple? If multiple, do they come off the stem at different places (**pinnately** or **feather compounded**) or do a number of them fan out from a single point on the stem (**palmately** or **fan compounded**)? Is each side rough, smooth, or hairy? What is the vein pattern? Is the leaf's outline smooth or toothed? If toothed, are there single teeth, or are they compound? What is the leaf's texture: thick, leathery, thin, hairy, smooth, shiny, dull?

To many, the most obvious feature of a leafless tree is its bark. Observe its color and texture, and whether you are looking at a young or a mature tree. Are there spines or thorns on the trunk or branches? Is the bark furrowed? Can you detect a pattern in the furrows? Does it peel horizontally or vertically? Are there spots in the bark (**lenticels**)? What shape, color, and texture are they?

If you can't be sure from the bark, look at the shape of the tree and its branches. Does the trunk go straight up, or does it divide and redivide? Which direction do branches grow from the trunk? Are branches straight, do they zigzag, or do they curve? Do twigs grow from a branch directly across from each other (**opposite branching**), or do they alternate on the branch (**alternate branching**)? Are they short and stout or thin and limber? In the winter, is there anything left hanging from the branches—berries (what color?), cones, dead leaves, or catkins? By being observant, you will be better prepared to make an identification. However, sometimes it is necessary to examine **buds** and **leaf scars** with a magnifying glass (see photo, page 245).

Despite these many detailed criteria, remember that there are only about 30 common trees in the Northeast that compose about 95 percent of those you'll see in the woods. Most can be learned simply by field observa-

Can you identify the four trees by looking at their branches overhead? Clue: they are growing in a marsh.

Proceeding clockwise, at one o'clock is a spruce, identifiable by its needles: it is a black spruce, because red spruce doesn't grow in wetlands. The next tree's long, tapering twigs grow opposite one another, providing the clue that it is a maple. Because it is growing in a marsh, it would be a red (or swamp) maple. The next tree also has opposite branching, but its twigs are much shorter than the maple's and have little or no taper; it's an ash. In the marsh, black ash is the best guess. The last tree, at twelve o'clock has finely tapering branches and twigs that are lacelike, with alternate (not opposite) branching: it's an elm. Because its roots are wet, it is almost certainly an American elm.

This is a good example of how both tree features—and knowledge of their habitats—aid identification.

tion, and nature walks—like those at Wilgus and Bald Mountain—are very helpful in acquiring this skill.

Getting There

Wilgus State Park is about a mile south of Ascutney on US 5. From the intersection of US 5 and Routes 12 and 131, go 1.3 miles south on US 5. The park entrance and parking lot are on the left.

Affiliated Organizations

Vermont Agency of Natural Resources, Department of Forests, Parks and Recreation (North Springfield office).

In the Area

Good views of the park, river, and the mountains of New Hampshire can be enjoyed by hiking up to The Pinnacle. The Pinnacle Trail starts across US 5 just north of the Wilgus parking lot. It follows an old road and then climbs through an oak/white pine forest to The Pinnacle (elev. 600 feet). The climb up is about a half mile in length, with a 250-foot elevation gain. To return, complete the loop on the blue-blazed trail, which winds back down to US 5 about a quarter of a mile north of the park entrance.

White River Junction Area

North Hartland Lake Nature Trail
North Hartland Lake

- 1 mile, some up and down
- 45 minutes
- moderate
- bring binoculars, hiking boots (may be muddy areas)

A very pleasant nature trail over hill and dale, with a large variety of ferns, mosses, wildflowers, and forests. There is a Watchable Wildlife Area at the dam.

North Hartland Lake was formed by the North Hartland Flood Control Dam, built downstream from Quechee Gorge on the Ottauquechee River. When the dam was built, it affected the water level of Dewey Pond in Quechee. The dam itself is 185 feet high. The high-water mark, at 135.83 feet, was set in 1987.

A **Watchable Wildlife Area** at the dam is part of the national program of identifying and highlighting

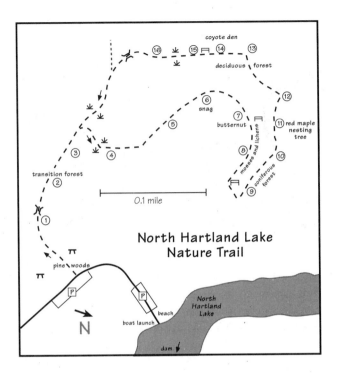

North Hartland Lake Nature Trail

areas accessible to the public for observing wildlife. From the top of the flood-control dam, an expanse of lake, open field, and forested edge unfolds below. **Migratory waterfowl, hawks, coyotes, mink, wild turkeys, whitetail deer,** and **songbirds** can be seen and heard. When we were there, the spillway was filled with **tree swallows** circling within its huge concrete confines. We watched their iridescent blue-black plumage glisten in the sun as they banked their turns at

The North Hartland Flood Control Dam.

the walls. Ravens nesting in the stone cliffs above scolded us with raucous croaks for disturbing them.

To reach the nature trail, follow the sign to the **George Perkins Marsh Conservation Area,** named after America's first outspoken conservationist (see page 267). A short distance beyond the pavilion, park in the pull-off area on the right. (If you continue down the road, it leads to the lake, boat launch, and beach area.) Cross the road and walk straight through the pine-forested picnic area to the trailhead.

Stop 1 is a footbridge and a thickly overgrown stream. **Newts, salamanders,** and **minnows** live in the stream, while **speckled alder** and **blackberry bushes** grow on its banks. Look for **Virginia creeper,** a climbing vine with five leaflets spreading from a single point. Such a leaf is called a **fan-** or **palmate-compound** leaf, because its structure is similar to a paper fan or the way fingers spread from the palm of a hand. When multiple leaflets grow from different points of a stem—like those of sumac, butternut, or ash—it is called a **feather-** or **pinnate-compound** leaf.

After a gentle climb, you are in a **transition forest** (Stop 2). Early succession species—including **quaking aspen** and **red maple**—are slowly being replaced by shade-tolerant species. At the next stop are white pine whose leaders were killed by the **white pine** weevil. They have branched and rebranched and are now commercially worthless **wolf trees.**

At a fork, a sign directs you to the right. The path follows a streambed for a short distance and then crosses it. At Stop 4 is a **mother log**—although it is decaying, it serves as a host to numerous organisms, insects, and vegetation, and can provide shelter for small animals. Insects and fungi invade the dead wood and transform it into nutrients that return to the soil. A **yellow birch sapling** is growing from the dead log, as is their habit. When decay eventually breaks down the log, the yellow birch will be left standing with its roots acting as stilts (see photo, page 312).

At Stop 5, the terrain is full of high and low spots created by trees blowing over. That rips their roots out of the ground and leaves a depression. When their trunks and roots decay, they leave a mound of organic matter. The **pit and mound topography** here is a sign that many trees have blown over. When standing trees die, they fall to the ground very slowly piece by piece. The fact that many blew over here is a clue that the soils are shallow or there is a high water table.

The standing dead tree at Stop 6 (a **snag**) is drier than one lying on the ground, so it lasts much longer. Many park managers simply call such trees **hazard trees** and cut them down, robbing porcupines, raccoon, mice, flying squirrels, woodpeckers, and other birds of important habitat. Like the fallen dead tree, this one is host to new seedlings as well.

The **butternut tree** at Stop 7 is a tree you've seen if you walked the Gordon Welchman or Pine Hill trails. It is intolerant of shade and seldom lives beyond 75 years. (By comparison, trees in the Black Gum Swamp and at Gifford Woods are more than 400 years old.)

Tree clubmoss, star moss, and **lichens** cover the ground at Stop 8. They grow year-round, and are the first plants to colonize unfavorable growing sites, such as bare rock. Lichens (see page 300) and mosses build up organic material while retaining moisture, creating favorable conditions for other plants. They create the velvety, carpetlike effect by their propensity for growing in colonies close together. After passing many such beds of moss, there is a bench and trail junction. If you continue straight, it is a shortcut back. To stay on the nature trail, turn left. This loop of the trail was laid out by Mark Rosenthal of the U.S. Army Corps of Engineers and built by Boy Scouts.

The evergreen **coniferous forest** at Stop 9 creates an inhospitable environment for most plants by blocking direct sunlight and raising the acidity of the soil as their needles slowly decay. Two plants that have adapted to this environment, however, are the **Canada mayflower** (the very common **wild lily-of-the-valley**) and **clintonia** (a short lily whose fruit is a dark blue or black beadlike berry).

At Stop 10 are several **hemlock saplings** beneath a heavy canopy of white pine. White pine is an **intermediate species** that invades open areas but can do well in partial shade. Hemlock is a **climax species,** able to seed and grow in complete shade, as it is here. Over time it will grow tall enough to shade and dominate the succession species that require light.

A **red maple** at Stop 11 has many cavities, though there is still a living branch or two at its top. The shape of the cavities depends on the woodpecker that created them. **Downy woodpeckers** create small circular holes; **hairy woodpeckers** create larger circular holes; and

A tree swallow built its nest in a cavity originally created by a pileated woodpecker.

Blackberry brambles bloom along the trail.

pileated woodpeckers create oval or elongated holes that can be a foot or more tall. Stop 12 is a paper birch among a stand of hemlock.

After passing into a stand of deciduous trees—**red maple, sugar maple, white ash, black birch,** and **yellow birch**—you come to Stop 13. This was pasture until about 40 years ago. When the land was purchased in the 1950s as part of the North Hartland Dam project, it was left undisturbed. After several phases of succession, its make-up is changing to that of a northern hardwood forest.

A small den in the earth is at Stop 14. The trail then traverses a hillside and leads to a bench at Stop 15—a wide drainage area that is perpetually damp. Here **trout-lilies** and **Goldie's, hayscented,** and **Christmas fern** cover the ground under deciduous trees, including **American elm.** At Stop 16, five additional ferns can be found: **bracken, maidenhair, marginal, interrupted,** and **sensitive.** We found **woodfern** along the trail as well. You then cross the brook on a footbridge and turn left at the next trail intersection, which leads to the end of the loop, where it joins the trail back to the picnic area.

George Perkins Marsh (1801–1882)

George Perkins Marsh was born not far from here — in Woodstock. He was the son of a congressman and a man of many interests and talents (including designing the Washington Monument). He was the first to describe in detail the destructive natural consequences of man's actions and to espouse a view that is the foundation of today's land and conservation ethic. In his landmark work, *Man and Nature,* he wrote:

> The earth is fast becoming an unfit home for its noblest inhabitant, and another era of equal human crime and human improvidence…would reduce it to such a condition of impoverished productiveness, of shattered surface, of climatic excess, as to threaten the depravation, barbarism, and perhaps even extinction of the species.

These words were written more than 130 years ago — in 1864! Long before Teddy Roosevelt, Marsh advocated the protection of forests, seeing that clear-cutting resulted in drying and erosion that destroyed the viability of waterways. He argued in flowery Victorian language that all of man's attempts to dominate the land — whether through damming rivers, digging canals, excessively clearing the land, planting in monocultures, or killing wildlife for sport — would result in destruction of the environment. By "barbarism," he meant primitive, natural beauty. He made his arguments in a global context. The ultimate question, to which his book's title refers, was whether men will act as creatures *of*, or *above*, nature.

The George Perkins Marsh Conservation Area reflects the U.S. Army Corps's agreement with his conservation philosophies. The area was dedicated to him on June 10, 1967, by Mrs. Lyndon (Lady Bird) Johnson.

Getting There

North Hartland Lake is located south of White River Junction in North Hartland. On US 5, go 4.2 miles north of the Hartland General Store. Just beyond the I-91 overpass, turn left on Clay Hill Road. (Coming from the north, look for Clay Hill Road on your right just before the overpass.) The access road to the dam is 1.1 miles on the right. It leads straight to the dam; a cutoff to the left leads to the nature trail parking.

Affiliated Organizations

U.S. Army Corps of Engineers, North Hartland Lake.

In the Area

Quechee Gorge is about 6 miles northwest of North Hartland on US 4.

Quechee Gorge
Quechee

- **view from the bridge or walk into gorge by several routes**
- **a 165-foot ascent if you enter the gorge**
- **10–60 minutes**
- **bring a camera**

A walk into and at the bottom of Vermont's most spectacular gorge. Quechee Gorge State Park and a great marsh for bird-watching are nearby.

It is hard to miss Quechee Gorge: a tourist gift shop, numerous cars pulled off the road, and people with cameras standing on the bridge are all sure signs that you've arrived at this "nature" walk. We won't mislead you—the only thing uniquely natural about this is the formation itself. But when you too pull over, walk out on the bridge, look at the **Ottauquechee River** 165 feet below (and run back to your car for your camera), you will find a descent to the bottom of the gorge irresistible.

From Quechee State Park (east of the bridge on the south side of US 4), there are several trails into the gorge. The most direct way down, however, is on the northeast corner of the bridge, next to the gift shop, where stairsteps lead to a trail. If you turn right, the path leads upstream to the picnic area and beyond to a

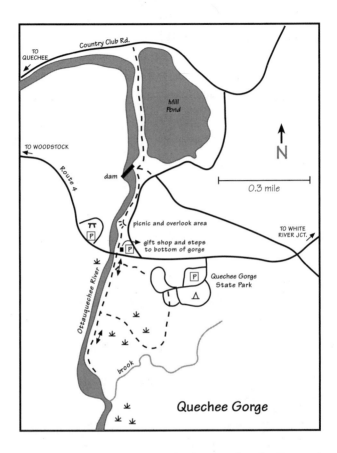

small waterfall at the site of what used to be **Dewey's Mill,** where fabric was made.

We turned left and walked a half-mile along the river to the end of the road-width trail. There, local kids were swimming and splashing in the deeper pools. We took our obligatory photos of each other framed by the gorge walls and bridge above. At the river's edge are such shrubs as **hobblebush, beaked willow, box-elder, wild currant, speckled alder,** and **witch-hazel.** The common trees along the gorge are **hemlock, beech, sugar** and **red maple, white** and **red pine,** and **yellow birch.**

We continued south for a way on the narrow footpath that leads into a marshy area of high grasses. The trail, however, does not follow the river's bank. Here there is more solitude and some great meadow and marsh bird-watching.

An alternative to going down the stairs at the bridge—one that makes more of a walk out of it—is to

Dewey's Mill Pond, where the waters rest peacefully before going over the dam to rush down the gorge.

begin at the state park and follow the blue-blazed loop to the river and back. It leaves the park near the wood-shed and reaches the river trail in a half-mile. This pleasant trail descends through steep woodlands, winds past a beaver pond, and bypasses two marshes filled with **ostrich ferns.** The return leg of the loop leaves the main trail just south of the bridge and climbs steeply back to the park in 0.2 mile.

How the Quechee Gorge Formed

Before the last ice sheet covered this area, the Ottauquechee River made a more gradual bend south-ward, about a mile east of its present course. In doing so, it passed around a rocky ridge, which US 4 now climbs as it heads east from the gorge. When Glacial Lake Hitch-cock formed (see page 66), the Ottauquechee River flowed into it. Its muddy waters began building up a huge delta of sand. The sand first filled its old riverbed and then continued piling up to an eventual depth of 170 feet, burying the ridge it had flowed around.

Then the dam of debris south of Hartford, Connecti-cut that had formed Lake Hitchcock gave way. As the waters ran out, they began quickly eroding the sediment at the lake's bottom, forming a waterfall. As the water-fall cut into the sediment, it moved northward. At this time, the Ottauquechee River was still flowing slowly over the wide sandy delta it had formed on top of the ridge. When the waterfall reached the Ottauquechee River, however, its waters began rushing out over the delta and carved a new bed some distance from its origi-nal one around the ridge. When the sandy sediment

The Ottauquechee River flows 165 feet below the Quechee Bridge.

eroded away, the river was left flowing over the metamorphic rock (**schist**) of the buried ridge. When you descend into the gorge today in five or 10 minutes, you can reflect upon the hundred centuries it took for the river to carve this gorge downward through the rock.

Getting There

Quechee Gorge cuts across US 4 between White River Junction and Woodstock. It is 5 miles west of White River Junction and 6 miles east of Woodstock.

Affiliated Organizations

Vermont Agency of Natural Resources, Department of Forests, Parks and Recreation (North Springfield office).

In the Area

From the bridge, turn left just past the gift shop onto Dewey's Pond Road. A picnic area is about a half-mile down on the left, overlooking a small waterfall at the mill dam. You can continue by foot or car to Dewey's Pond—a good place to spot waterfowl. Dewey's Mill closed operations here and moved to New Hampshire in 1962 as a result of the North Hartland Dam (see page 260). In 1936, the mill was producing 30,000 yards of fabric per week—some of which was used to make New York Yankee and Boston Red Sox uniforms.

Eshqua Bog
Town of Hartland

- all trails combined, less than 0.5 mile
- 30 minutes
- very easy (Northern Loop Trail moderate)
- bring wildflower identification book, magnifying glass

A boardwalk through the middle of the bog provides a close look at its many wildflowers, heaths, sedges, and carnivorous plants. Species along the walk are identified.

The trail circles the 40-acre area, with a boardwalk passing through the middle of the bog. On the right, shortly after passing the entrance sign, **partridgeberry** and **goldthread** (named for the color of its root threads) can be seen; both are evergreen plants. Partridgeberry fruit is red and edible and a favorite of **grouse.** Down the path, bordered by **cattails,** is a sign-in box for visitors. Here there is a choice between entering the boardwalk or continuing straight on the north loop; we couldn't resist the boardwalk.

On either side of the boardwalk are many **showy lady's-slippers.** Visit in June or July to see this orchid's extravagant purple-and-white bloom on its one-to-three-foot stem. One sight of it in bloom and it is clear why it is known as the largest and most beautiful orchid

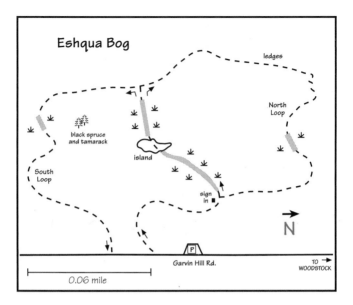

Eshqua Bog

ledges

North Loop

black spruce and tamarack

island

South Loop

sign in ■

N

P

Garvin Hill Rd.

TO WOODSTOCK

0.06 mile

in the north. As the boardwalk nears the hummock island in the middle, there are **false hellebore, bunchberry,** and **scouring rush.** Scouring rushes, or **horsetails,** are the most primitive of ferns. They are direct descendants of the tree-sized ferns that grew in Pangea 300 million years ago.

In a moment, you feel the softness of compressed peat and organic matter under your feet as you step onto the island. **Bunchberry** and **sarsaparilla** grow here, and as you gaze about, you easily come to appreciate the incredible diversity supported by this fen. It isn't known how many such fens, bogs, and wetlands were lost in the past when they were drained by settlers anxious to get a crop in without having to clear forest.

As the second boardwalk leads back to dry land, you pass **clustered snakeroot, purple avens, Labrador-tea,** carnivorous **pitcher-plants** (see North Springfield Bog, page 227) and **round-leafed sundews** (see page 279). Back on land, the trail around the north end of the bog climbs a steep ledge above the bog. At the top are several massive sugar maples. They are still alive, but there are many large cavities where branches once protruded and incredible whorls in the bark from healed wounds inflicted long ago. Below them are sawdust from the drilling of **pileated woodpeckers**—the Woody Woodpecker woodpecker. As we walked the trail, a

One of nature's most outrageous displays, the showy lady's-slipper greets visitors near the beginning of the boardwalk.

pair of them were staking out their respective territories by drumming back and forth. A pileated's drumming can be recognized by its loudness and a slower pace than that of the hairy or downy woodpecker; the tapping slows, descending in pitch, at the end. Their shrill call is similar in cadence to the drumming, and is about the loudest birdcall you'll hear in the woods.

The trail off the ledge is steep and narrow. At the foot of the ledge, it crosses a boardwalk over the outlet stream. Eshqua Bog is technically a **fen,** because an inlet stream brings fresh water that adds nutrients to its environment and reduces its natural acidity. The only source of water in a true **bog** is precipitation and runoff. Near the stream are **marsh-marigold** and **bloodroot,** whose orange-red sap is—like all members of the poppy family—poisonous. Although wildflower guides attribute its common name to the color of its sap, Native Americans used the juice pressed from its roots as a red war-paint and dye.

To reach the southern loop, cross through the middle of the bog again. As I walked the boardwalk from the island a second time, a **marsh wren** was startled out from underneath it. This time, turn left at its end. Typical wetland trees grow out of the fen: **black spruce** and **larch,** sometimes called **tamarack** (see Big Trees, page 171). Native Americans used its roots to sew together their birch-bark canoe coverings, and its strong, water-resistant wood has long been used in boatbuilding.

This path crosses the fen's inlet stream on a boardwalk and just past it, on the right, are **painted trillium.** After we passed through a stand of yellow birch, we emerged on the road. There we watched a **yellow-bel-**

lied sapsucker drilling holes horizontally around a tree, the red of his crown and throat a blur as he worked.

Round-Leafed Sundews

Like pitcher-plants, **sundews** have evolved a unique means of obtaining the nitrogen they need. Often found near pitcher-plants, they are small and unobtrusive. The round-leafed sundew has a reddish tint to it. Its half-inch leaves are covered with hairs that secrete droplets of a sticky substance, making the plant look as if it is covered with small dewdrops. When insects land on the leaves, they stick to them. The leaf then slowly curls

The tiny, inch-high sundew awaits an unsuspecting insect, which it will entrap.

around the victims and digests them. They bloom from June to August with small white or pink flowers at the top of a four-to-nine-inch stem.

Getting There

Eshqua Bog is south of Woodstock. US 4 makes a sharp right just before it enters Woodstock Village from the east (at the Richmond Ford/Mobil Gas station). At its turn, take a left up Hartland Hill Road. At 1.2 miles, shortly after passing a log house on the right, bear right onto a dirt road (there is no sign, but it is Garvin Hill Road). At another 1.2 miles, a sign on the right marks the bog's entrance. Just before the sign is an area to park along the road.

Affiliated Organizations

Owned and managed by The Nature Conservancy's Vermont chapter and the New England Wild Flower Society.

Communities Nature Trail
Vermont Institute of Natural Science (VINS), Woodstock

- **0.9 mile, 200-foot elevation gain (the Pond Loop Trail avoids the steep gain)**
- **1 hour**
- **moderate (Pond Loop alone is easy)**

This beautiful walk passes a pond and field to climb to a view west. It follows a ridge and emerges at a spectacular high point in a meadow.

Look for the sign at the end of the parking lot to locate the information bulletin board and booklets for the three color-coded self-guided walks. The Communities Nature Trail, blazed in blue, illustrates the interdependence of groups of plants and animals that live in one place, mutually supported by the energy and resources available. We turned left past the bulletin board to begin our walk along the pond.

The predators at the **Raptor Center** behind you add their calls and screeches to those of the songbirds found near the pond. Many people stood around silently with binoculars pointed off into the distance, while top-gun **tree swallows** whipped around above the pond in an impressive display of aerobatics as they snapped insects out of the air. Spaced around the pond are what look like long badminton nets. These are used to snare birds for

Communities Nature Trail

the ongoing **VINS bird banding program** (see page 287). On the right, a demonstration garden shows plants that attract birds to one's yard. We followed the grassy trail along a stone fencerow and across a large field.

If you do not feel like climbing to the top of the ridge you see rising across the pond, then turn right on the **Pond Loop Trail** where it is marked. This *easy* trail circles the pond on a level path.

Stop 3 is the stone wall. Virtually every walk in this book follows such a stone wall at one point or another, hard evidence that 75 percent of Vermont was once pasture or farmland. The rocks were hauled out of the field, where they had lain for more than 10,000 years since they were dropped by the glacier. Such **glacial erratics** are chunky and uneven, and it takes careful attention to dry-wall construction principles for a wall to remain intact through a century or two of frost heave and penetration by tree roots. **Ostrich fern, interrupted fern,** and **lady fern** prefer the moist nooks and crannies of such a wall.

At the corner of the field, marked by several **butternut** trees, the Gordon Welchman Nature Trail (page 289), blazed yellow, cuts off to the left. We continued straight, following blue blazes. We entered a stand of white pine as the trail began its climb. It has the regular spacing of a plantation. The stand has been extensively

Above the VINS pond rises a meadow, bordered by the pine plantation.

pruned to increase the flow of air around their trunks. That promotes healthier trees and provides clear lumber when they are milled — greatly increasing their value. The slash from the pruning has been left to decay and return nutrients to the soil.

The climb is rather steep, and the pine needles underfoot can be slippery. We took our time and were plenty thankful for the bench at Stop 9, where we sat to enjoy the view west. In the distance are **Shrewsbury Peak** (elev. 3,720 feet) on the left and **Killington** (elev. 4,241 feet) on the right. Their summits are exposures of the oldest rock in New England (see page 114).

The pines were planted in 1950. We were climbing the hillside through the stand when I stopped for a second because I sensed something had changed. At first I didn't know what, but then I realized it was the trees; we were still in a stand of pine, but now they were **red pine** rather than white. If a child had been along, she no doubt would have been picking up pinecones and noticing that suddenly there were small round ones instead of long skinny ones. The bark of the red pine is redder and flakier than that of white pine. Study the bark of each type and you'll easily be able to tell the difference at a glance in the future. The needles are also a dead giveaway: both are long but red pine has two needles to a cluster while white pine has five.

We came to a small stand of **quaking aspen.** It appeared to me that there must have been early mortality in this section of pines and the aspen quickly invaded. The trail curves left and climbs to the top of the ridge. The ground at Stop 10 is covered by **star moss** and **reindeer lichen. Blackberries, milkweed,** and **hardwood**

saplings are all taking advantage of the direct sunlight in the clearing. The trail then leads to the top of the ridge, where you are invited to use a rope hand-guide to walk with your eyes closed and focus on hearing and smell. We would love to tell you how the sound of the wind in the pines affected us, but the air was absolutely still. If a chickadee hadn't been calling, the only sound we could have reported would have been an airplane.

Along the northern side of the ridge, at Stop 14, is **common barberry.** Its fruit is eaten by birds only as a last resort and its spines protect it from being browsed by **herbivores,** such as deer, so its berries often remain at winter's end. Stop 15 is a quiz: a white pine and a red pine are on either side of the trail. Can you tell which is which?

We then emerged from the forest into a meadow 200 feet above VINS. We sat on a bench to enjoy the views and birds and beauty. In the distance, rising sharply above the rolling green hills, stands Mt. Ascutney (see page 238). Here you'll want to reach for your binoculars.

The plants growing in the meadow provide clues to the earlier use of the land. The **dwarf juniper** and **hawthorn** shrubs are more developed than the other plants in the meadow — that means animals used to graze here. Why? Because livestock graze just about everything in sight — except, that is, for juniper (because of its very sharp, stiff needles) and hawthorn (because of its long thorns). When a pasture is abandoned, the juniper and hawthorn are already well established.

To an ecologist, this meadow would be referred to as a combination of **edge habitat** and a **shrub meadow.** Edge habitat generally supports about three times more wildlife than do deep woods and it can have 10 or 20 times the plant diversity. A meadow offers as much as 30 times more food per acre than does a forest. Because these regions are so rich in protection, nesting sites, sunny warmth, early snowmelt, and food, they attract a great variety of birds and wildlife.

The **American woodcock,** for example, needs open space as a runway in order to take off. And speaking of runways, **meadow voles** have probably created 10 or more miles of runways in this meadow by chewing down grasses and eating them. They consume more than half their body weight in plant material a day, and a female can produce as many as a million offspring in her lifetime. The **hawks** circling overhead in the day and the **owls** at night are part of this community. They play their role by keeping the voles in check, preventing the meadow from being mowed bare by these busy little rodents. The interrelationships in this meadow are beyond count, but the complex balance—from deep in the earth to high in the sky—is a reflection that life establishes *communities* we can never understand if we look upon them as mere *collections.*

We moved on to a **sweetbrier rosebush (eglantine)** with a very unusual gall on it: the **mossy rose gall.** It looked like a large clump of golden moss. In the spring, the gall houses the growing larvae of the **mossy rose gall wasp.** They emerge as wasps, who then lay eggs on the sweetbrier. When the larvae hatch, they create a gall in which to overwinter.

We then started downward as steeply as we originally climbed. We greatly enjoyed this walk (especially the meadow). As we neared the pond, Patti spotted a

The mossy rose gall.

pileated woodpecker we had heard drumming and calling during the walk. She watched a long time with binoculars as he enlarged a cavity looking for his favorite meal of carpenter ants.

The Bird Banding Program at VINS

The fine-meshed mist nets along the pond can't be seen by birds in the early morning light. From late April through October they are used to capture birds. Their species, age, sex, and date and place of banding are recorded and forwarded to the Department of the Interior, National Biological Survey, which licenses all banding stations. A thin band of aluminum bearing a unique serial number is placed around one of the bird's legs before it is released.

The data collected provides insight into the size and nature of bird populations, migration habits, and the effects of weather and other environmental factors. Changes in populations can be early indicators of environmental changes. For instance, the near absence of singing birds in towns that had sprayed DDT was revealed in Rachel Carson's classic book, *Silent Spring*. This showed us the dangers of using long-lived pesticides that collect in the body fat of animals. (With thanks to the authors of the *Communities Trail Guide*.)

Getting There

VINS is located southwest of the village of Woodstock. Circle the Woodstock Green on US 4, and, at its southwestern corner, turn right onto Church Hill Road. Proceed 1.7 miles and the VINS entrance will be on your right.

Affiliated Organizations

Vermont Institute of Natural Science, Bragdon Nature Preserve (no pets allowed).

In the Area

While at VINS, visit the **Raptor Center**—a living museum that introduces visitors to the raptors of northern New England. The outdoor museum houses 26 species of owls, hawks, and eagles in spacious flight habitats. All the birds have permanent injuries that prevent their successful return to the wild. A fee is charged for entry to the Raptor Center. A second VINS trail, the Gordon Welchman Nature Trail, follows on the next page.

Gordon Welchman Nature Trail

Vermont Institute of Natural Science (VINS), Woodstock

- 1–1.5 miles (ups and downs, very steep to marsh)
- 1–2 hours (depending on choice of route)
- moderate/difficult
- bring binoculars, magnifying glass, good walking shoes

A ridge walk that is unique and inspiring, with an abundance of plants and birds and a view of the Ottauquechee Valley. The trail then drops to a marsh, where plant species are identified.

VINS does a superb job of creating guides to its trails, available at the bulletin board located at the far right of the parking lot, where all trails begin. Written by Michael Caduto, the guide to this trail emphasizes the interrelationships among living things and their environment. We are not reproducing the guide's abundant information here; rather, we will share our experience and observations on the walk.

The first leg of the Gordon Welchman Nature Trail is the same as that of the Communities Trail and can be consulted there (page 281). The trail is blazed in yellow. Several large **butternut trees** (see page 244) stand at the

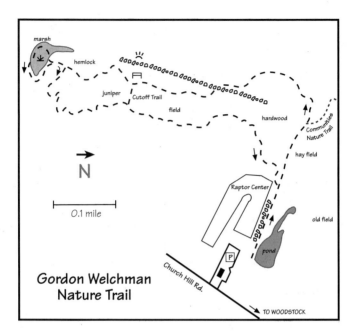

Gordon Welchman Nature Trail

N

0.1 mile

TO WOODSTOCK

trail junction where the trail turns south from the Communities Trail. Their heavy branches grow out over the field, but few grew into the hillside forest behind it. That means the trees developed with their backs in shade. From that, we know that the forest behind them existed since the butternuts began growing here.

Butternut (**white walnut**) is related to **black walnut** and is easy to recognize by its bark, but to confirm it, look at its **leaf scars** (where leaf stems once were attached to the twig). On many trees, these scars are small, but those of the butternut's stout, knobby twigs are large and easy to see. To me, each scar looks like the face of an organ-grinder's monkey, little cap and all (see photo, page 245). The three dots that make up the face of the monkey are called **bundle scars**—an important clue to identifying tree families. Butternut is also the only large tree commonly seen in this region whose twigs have chambered pith.

Later in the day, as we returned past the pond at the end of our walk, we heard a strange, continuous, high-pitched scraping sound. We stopped to look around, and finally I spotted a **red squirrel** on a fence post by the stone wall. He was holding a butternut between his forepaws and avidly chewing through its

On a foggy morn, the trail on top of the ridge reminds one of Nova Scotia or the British Isles.

thick outer shell. It was May, so it had to be a nut he had squirreled away last fall and just recently retrieved. Butternuts and walnuts are preferred by squirrels above everything else, despite the work it takes to gnaw through their thick woody shell several times just to get at the different chambers of nutmeat. In one experiment, scientists planted 420 black walnuts a foot deep in a multiacre field. Within six weeks, squirrels had located and run off with 419 of them. They replant the nuts for winter storage and—thank goodness—don't always remember where they buried them all. This is an effective strategy for the tree to disperse its large, heavy seeds. If it weren't for the squirrels, the only place nuts would grow is under nut-bearing trees.

Up the old farm road in the forest, as I photographed a giant burl on a sugar maple, a **meadow vole** popped its head out of a hole to watch Patti walk by. Under the leaves, we could see that his burrow was among the roots of a long-decayed stump. We continued uphill through a beech forest, most of which, unfortunately, showed different stages of beech bark disease (see page 251). Very little grows in the understory of such a forest, giving it a spacious, airy feeling. At the top of the ridge, two **lichen moths** (*Lycomorpha pholus*)—danced in the air above our heads, the yellow at the base of their dark wings catching the sunlight. They feed on the many lichens covering the stone wall at the edge of the woods.

Lichens on the wall include **pixie cups, British soldiers, worm lichen,** and **orange star** (once you've heard its name, you'll have no trouble identifying it). Looked at close up, lichens create strange, exotic landscapes

British soldiers, or redcoats — a lichen.

that, in their own way, can be as beautiful as a meadow of flowers. To appreciate them, however, you need to look very closely, and that requires magnification. I use a 5x loupe. It is small and light and easy to keep in my shirt pocket. I use it constantly, whether to see fern spores, bud scales, bundle scars, tiny critters, leaf surfaces, moss leaves, lichens, or the incredible palette with which nature has decorated the backs of bugs. By using a lens, you get to explore two worlds on one walk!

The trails here (thus far) are a perfect balance between constructed trails and the more natural feeling of woodland and meadow paths. In this meadow atop the ridge, we came to the first of several benches and sat, taking in the world around us. It was a beautiful spring day, with deep blue skies and puffy cumulus clouds. Killington and Shrewsbury peaks rose in the distance at the end of the Ottauquechee River Valley. This bench was given in memory of Emma Lou Rothman, "who always stopped here for the views." So beautiful is this spot that Patti and I began discussing how much better a memory something like this is than a carved granite stone.

My eyes were drawn to the stone wall at the field's edge. I looked at each stone and imagined the farmer who, with a **hornbeam** lever, pried each one out of the ground (old-timers called *Ostrya virginiana* "lever-wood"). Then he and his sons manhandled it onto a stone sled. An ox pulled the sled to the wall, where they again manhandled the stones into position. I could see from the wall's construction, though, that this wall builder of yore was a different kind of man from many of those who cleared land. Most drywalls were thrown up by men in a hurry to get the land cleared and the crops in. At this farm, I'm sure the lower field was cleared first, and the wall adjoining it near the pond was built like thousands of others. But once that land was cleared and the winter stores were assured, the farmer — or one of his succeeding sons or grandsons — came up to this meadow and decided to take his time.

The builder held back the heaviest stones until the sides of the wall were built up. Then, with a lot of help, he lifted the largest stones several feet off the ground and placed them on top of the wall as capstones. Having "rock 'n' rolled" a little myself — enough to know the weight of those stones and how they feel when you set one down on your finger — I know the time and effort he put into his wall. He must have loved this place as much as we do today to have built such beautiful and enduring walls on this far hilltop—especially when the only ones around likely to appreciate his work were sheep.

We came to two more benches and a sign indicating the **Cutoff Trail** to the left. By taking it, you can continue to explore this upper meadow or return to the Raptor Center. In either case, you avoid the steep *difficult* trip down to the marsh and back up.

We passed the Cutoff Trail and began to snake through a solid carpet of **dwarf juniper.** The afternoon sun was shining on the valley, falling on the juniper's blue berries and making the pink and white and orange quartz stones in the wall glow as if from within. **Quartzite** stones were broken away from here by the glacier and carried away. Thousands of years later, it dropped them all over the landscape for miles south of here. By now, many people have picked them up and used them in their rock gardens—a work of pleasure compared with the farmer who had to move the sons of guns out of his pasture. On the left, the sunlight fell on a patch of **reindeer lichen** and created a fascinating pattern of shadows and structure. The fact that it hadn't been grazed is a good indication that there are very few reindeer about.

The trail then entered a hemlock forest and we began to descend to the marsh. A **hairy woodpecker** called, but his voice was almost drowned out by the sound of our feet crunching hemlock cones like popcorn. Take our word for it: this trail involves more than just a little bad footing. It is a very steep descent on slippery leaves and needles that follows a deer trail. If you are not up to the climb down and back up, return the short distance back to the Cutoff Trail. It brings you to a choice of turning left to return to VINS or turning right to explore more of this ridgetop.

We hiked carefully down the slope to a trail junction, where a yellow arrow points uphill to the left—the return leg of the trip. A series of pressure-treated steps lower down leads to the boardwalk through the marsh. This glacially created depression was full of water thousands of years ago, but has been filled in by leaves and twigs and needles. Today it is in the final stages of succession as a **tree swamp**. It supports **American elm, red maple, black spruce, black ash, willow,** and **eastern hemlock**—all commonly found where there is a high water table. The **white pine** and **yellow birch** that struggle to grow from the higher hummocks represent the next stage of succession getting its start. In a couple of hundred more years, this will just be a moist area in a hardwood forest.

I craned my neck upward to see the tree crowns and branches against the sky. Knowing how a tree grows helps to identify it in winter. One of the most beautiful branch patterns is here—**American elm** (variously called **white elm** and **water elm**). Its twigs truly zigzag and before the leaves come out, its alternating buds are spaced so closely that the twigs look beaded. They are so very long and slender that when you look up through the leafless branches, you see far more sky than tree. The twigs branch out very evenly and are widely spaced, so the overall effect reminds me of lace—but a lace created by a draftsman with a very sharp pencil and a good straightedge.

The VINS staff helpfully labeled a number of the trailside plants, and that could only be improved by labeling even more of them. (To learn more about life in marshes, fens, and bogs, see Healing Springs, page 1, North Springfield Bog, page 223, and Eshqua Bog, page 275.)

At the end of the boardwalk, Patti flushed out a **ruffed grouse.** We started uphill on the trail we had descended. At the trail junction, we turned right, following the yellow arrow. A short distance up that trail on the left was a dead beech tree. On it were several of the **largest white shelf fungi** I've ever seen. As VINS naturalist Steve Faccio wryly said of them, "Quite a specimen."

We crested the ridge and started on a breathtaking stretch of trail. The almost solid cover of dwarf juniper, interspersed with occasional birch and pine, is so beautiful that it would make an honest landscaper give up trying. Buried amongst the juniper on a short spur trail is exposed bedrock whose incredible pattern of folded sedimentary layers would likewise make a Zen stone gardener give up trying to improve on nature.

The way the narrow path wound through the juniper reminded us of walks at Nova Scotia's Cape Breton. At one point, however, when we glanced back from the path, a beautiful framed view of Mt. Ascutney anchored us once again in Vermont. A flock of **cedar waxwings** fluttered about us from limb to limb until they flew together into the juniper where they promptly disappeared but did not quiet down. Only female junipers have berries, and their popularity with birds is well understood by gin drinkers, since juniper berries are used to flavor gin.

The pattern of this outcropping of rock reveals the fluid forces that formed it.

Several low and heavily branched, open-grown sugar maples, probably approaching their second century in age, are framed against the high-meadow sky. The stone wall on the right is—like the one on the other side of the field—buttressed with immense capstones. It makes me wonder how many yards of stone wall surround this field and how long it took the farmer to build them (or did he have a dozen sons in the days when people commonly sired their laborers?).

Near an apple tree and a fallen butternut, I spotted a **large cavity** in an old sugar maple to the right. Its bark had been freshly chewed away for a foot around the opening. I puzzled over that for a moment, and then I could see it...It was a subzero night in February...the

The cavity in the sugar maple whose occupant ate the bark.

high winds blew across the mouth of the cavity, creating a relentless mind-numbing roar…there was no way to get warm, and without food, the end was in sight…."Do I have to climb out of my den in this weather," it asked itself, "…wander around in the dark…find a hemlock tree…climb 40 or 50 feet up its frozen slippery bark…walk out on a slender limb in this howling wind and driving snow…? No way," it decided. "I'm eating home tonight."

It stuck its head out of the cavity and began gnawing off the sugar maple bark. "Yuck! It's awful compared with the tips of hemlock branches," it thought, "but it sure beats having to go out to dinner on a night like this."

I walked over to the tree and there, below the cavity, was an enormous pile of scat that confirmed my guess about its messy occupant: Mr. Porcupine.

Downhill through a hemlock wood, there are a lot of snags. As I always do, I softly scratched each one, hoping to see a flying squirrel poke his head out of a cavity. No luck. However, I found a day-glo lime-green tennis ball in the litter at the base of one tree, and all of the fuzz on its exposed side was gone. Either someone was very hungry, or somewhere — either in one of those cavities or in a ground burrow — there is a very colorful nest.

And with that, we regained the trail back to the pond. As we returned past the pond at the end of our walk, we heard a strange, continuous, high-pitched scraping sound...

Lichens

Lichens consist of a mutual and necessary relationship between two plants: an **alga** and a **fungus.** The alga — usually a single-cell green alga — creates food from sunlight via photosynthesis, while the fungus provides shelter and absorbs minerals from rainwater, dew, and — by producing an acid — dissolves them from the rock itself. To remember this unique plant association, use the phrase: *A fungus takes a "lichen" to an alga.*

Though there is some overlap, lichens are of three general types: **crusty lichens,** like the orange star, grow flat on rocks or trees; **leaf-like lichens** are only attached in one spot — like the gray-green **pale shield lichen** that grow on trees; and **shrubby lichens,** like British soldiers and reindeer lichen, that grow by branching. Extracts from a few lichens are used in making antibiotics, and a dye from lichens is used to color wool in Harris tweeds.

They are among the slowest growing of all plants and can endure lengthy dry periods. The average lichen lives to be 100 to 200 years old. Although they continue to photosynthesize, even when the temperature is below freezing, they need light. Thus, lichens don't grow on the part of the tree that is covered with snow — making it a good indicator of average snow depth in a forest. And for all of its longevity, it is very sensitive. Scientists use lichens to study air quality, because they react to even small amounts of pollutants. If you see healthy lichens, you know you're breathing fresh, clean air.

Getting There

VINS is located southwest of the Village of Woodstock. Circle the Woodstock Green on US 4, and, at its southwestern corner, turn right onto Church Hill Road. Proceed 1.7 miles, and the VINS entrance will be on your right.

Affiliated Organizations

Vermont Institute of Natural Science, Bragdon Nature Preserve (no pets allowed).

In the Area

For more information, see Communities Nature Trail, page 288.

Amity Pond
Pomfret

- **0.5 mile (with more than 2 miles of additional trails)**
- **30 minutes**
- **very easy**

This walk offers a beautiful hilltop view, several different ecosystems, and an interesting water conservation project. In addition, there is a lovely story on how the pond became known as Amity.

When we entered the Amity Pond area in April, we heard a deafening chorus of **wood frogs** coming from a small pond and several vernal pools near the entrance. Taking the trail to our left, we approached the pond. Of course the hundreds of frogs hushed and dove for the muddy bottom. We sat quietly on the bank for a few minutes, and soon they all rose again to the surface. There they floated — arms and legs outstretched — hanging almost motionless in the water. Soon they started up their chorus again. Every once in a great while, one would suddenly dart at another. We'd see only a quick splash of water and then they'd swim away to float quietly again. A photo taken of the splash later revealed that they both dove underwater during their extremely brief encounter.

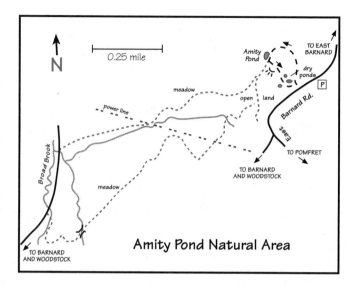

N

0.25 mile

TO EAST
BARNARD

Amity
Pond

dry
ponds

P

meadow

open   land

Power line

Barnard Rd.

East

TO POMFRET

Broad Brook

TO BARNARD
AND WOODSTOCK

meadow

Amity Pond Natural Area

TO BARNARD
AND WOODSTOCK

A little farther up this spur is one of several camping shelters on the property. Each provides total privacy and offers an amenity—a view, a water feature, or an open meadow. In front of this one is a **dry pond.** It and several others on the property are designed to catch and hold the water from snowmelt and spring rains. They are usually full—or even overflowing—by May. Rather than running off in streams and journeying to the ocean, the water collects in them and slowly percolates back into the ground. People in the area say that they think these pools have already helped raise the local water table. It is also hoped that the ponds will bring back to life a brook that once ran through the property but is now dry.

Returning on the spur, we followed a sign to the field. On our right was a stand of **bigtooth aspen.** The trunks of younger trees and the branches of more mature ones have a light green bark tinged with orange. The trail, as wide as a road and maintained as a cross country ski trail in the winter, leads up to an open meadow, cutting through a stone wall at a line of old sugar maples. A **view** to the west pulls one forward into the meadow. There, a small hardened limestone out-cropping provides a natural vantage point, from which the tops of Pico and Killington Mountains can be seen. When we looked down on the outcropped stone, we saw a number of **dried scat,** most likely that of red fox (see page 306).

A wood frog greets us at Amity Pond.

When we walked across the meadow to this vantage point, we passed another grove of bigtooth aspen behind a small ridge on the right. They surround the now hidden Amity Pond — which is only about 25 by 40 feet in size and perhaps more accurately described as a large pool. And here's a lovely story: it is said that two young ladies, attending the East Barnard school, vowed lifelong friendship. But when one married a Pomfret man and the other a Barnard man, they were separated. They corresponded during the year, but each summer they would set aside a day and both would hike up the hill from their respective towns and share a picnic by this tiny pond — and thus it became known as Amity Pond.

Across the meadow from the pond is a break in the stone wall where the trail leads back past the shelter to the entrance. A letter from Elizabeth and Dick Brett of Woodstock dated July 1969 is posted at the shelter. It reads, in part:

> To our friends and neighbors,
>
> In our mechanical world there is a forgotten man. The man who likes quiet relaxation, free from the noise and smell of machines. There is no place where people can walk, snowshoe, ski, or ride horseback free from all-purpose vehicles, trail bikes, snowmobiles, etc....To provide a place where a limited number of people can be free of machines for a brief spell, Elizabeth and I have deeded our Amity Pond land in the State of Vermont to be used as a park....It is our hope that this park may be a true refuge. It is our hope that the

sportsmanship of those who travel by machine will permit this small area to be a sanctuary for wildlife, native plants, and the people who cherish these things in an atmosphere of quiet relaxation.

"Scat Happens"

As wildlife biologists are heard to say: *scat happens.* When you see scat in an important place, like on a rock in the middle of a trail or on a high point (as at the vantage point at Amity Pond), you can be pretty sure that it was left there by one of three animals: a **fox, coyote,** or **bobcat.** All three are drawn to prominent places to leave their mark.

Scat from a fox on a summer diet of insects, berries, and plants.

It is difficult to distinguish among the scat of these three animals. Fox scat is generally from two to four inches long and only a half-inch in diameter, while coyote scat is closer to an inch in diameter and may be longer. In the winter, fox scat is filled with hair and usually longer, with points at each end. In summer months, when its diet tends toward berries and insects, its scat is shorter, blunter, and softer.

It is impossible to make a certain identification of bobcat scat and therefore difficult to distinguish it from either of the other two. The size of bobcat scat and its diet overlap them both. In Vermont, however, the larger number of fox and the return of the eastern coyote makes either of them the better guess.

Getting There

Amity Pond is tucked away near East Barnard. Take Route 12 north out of Woodstock. In 1.2 miles, follow the sign to Pomfret by bearing right onto South Pomfret Road. At the South Pomfret Post Office, bear right at the fork. In 4.7 miles, in an area called Hewetts Corners, the road bears right. Just after the curve, turn left toward Sharon on Howe Hill Road. In 0.3 mile, turn left onto the unpaved East Barnard Road. In 2.3 miles, at the very crest of the hill, park on the right where there is space for four or five cars. The entrance to the Amity Pond Natural Area is marked by a sign on the left. No radios or powered vehicles of any kind are allowed.

Affiliated Organizations

Amity Pond is a Natural Area managed by the Vermont Agency of Natural Resources, Department of Forests, Parks and Recreation (North Springfield office).

In the Area

As the map indicates, there is an additional 2.7-mile loop trail that includes some road walking. The landscape is a mix of meadows and forest. However, as can be seen from Amity Pond, most of the trail heads downhill, requiring a long uphill walk to return. In several places the trail is quite steep. In the winter, this trail is part of the Skyline Cross-Country Ski Trail that runs between Woodstock and Pomfret.

Hurricane Forest Wildlife Refuge Park
Town of Hartford

- **1.7 miles total; loops range from 0.2 to 0.8 mile**
- **15 minutes–1.5 hours**
- **very easy/moderate**

A beautiful series of trails through stands of old-growth white pine, a number of which blew down in the hurricane of 1938. A woodland brook runs through the watershed.

We began at the upper entrance, where a monument honors Winsor and Bertha Brown, who donated this land to the town of Hartford to be kept perpetually in its wild and natural state. The 142-acre forest is also a year-round wildlife sanctuary, with no hunting, shooting, or trapping allowed.

We entered the park and crossed a small footbridge to a trail junction. There we turned left and walked down the Creek Trail to its junction with the Beacon Hill Loop, where a hand-hewn bench sat near the cascading brook. We turned right on the 0.8-mile Beacon Hill Loop. We ascended the crest of the hill on a series of switchbacks. These trails were built in 1992 by the Hartford Boy Scouts and Youth Conservation Corps. They are beautifully laid out and constructed, with

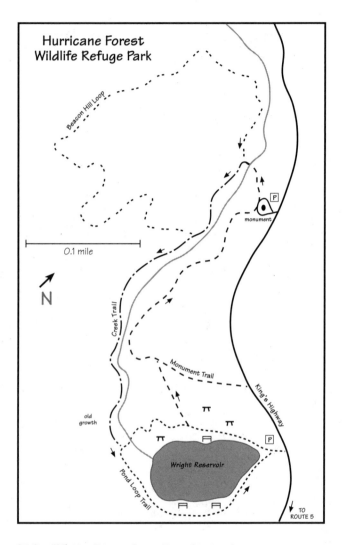

Hurricane Forest
Wildlife Refuge Park

Beacon Hill Loop

P

monument

0.1 mile

N

Creek Trail

Monument Trail

King's Highway

old
growth

Pond Loop Trail

P

Wright Reservoir

TO
ROUTE 5

some of the best blazing and signage of any we've walked. Benches on this climb have been placed at the very points where we wanted to stop and rest.

As we traversed the sloping hillside, three **whitetail deer** bounded out of the woods and cut across the path 30 feet in front of us. They continued downhill, while we started uphill again, glad for the brief encounter. Several vistas open up on the left as the trail continued upward. We crossed the hilltop through a forest of birch, oak, cherry, and maple mixed with tall pines and hemlocks. We stopped for a minute to examine winter **red fox scat** (see page 306) left prominently on the trail. Then we descended into an area of **old-growth,** with white pines rising 60 feet or more to their first branch. We also passed an exceptionally tall **red oak** on the right, its trunk so straight it looked like it had used a plumb bob to grow.

The trail then descends and dramatically enters a stand of **paper birch.** The forest floor is covered with **princess pine** and **Christmas** and **cinnamon ferns.** Soon the sound of the brook drowned out the birdsongs. We passed a stone wall and rejoined the Creek Trail. We continued straight on the 0.4-mile long **Creek Trail,** which connects to the Pond Loop.

The trail leads gradually downhill along the creek bank. Ferns filled the glades, and mosses covered the stones in the valley to our left. On our right were the first of many giant fallen trees. These old-growth pine were toppled by the hurricane of September 21, 1938, but that was not the event after which the park was named. The forest's namesake was a hurricane that struck sometime between 1761 and 1800.

Sunlight filtered through the trees and was absorbed by the dark-green mosses covering the slowly decaying trunks of these giants. There are some very good examples here of the propensity **yellow birch** has for seeding on fallen trees and stumps. As their host slowly decays, they are left standing on stilted roots.

We walked downhill and passed through a stone wall to where **old-growth white pines** are still standing. This area is lower on the hillside, so it must protect them better from high winds. If this hill acquired its name from a hurricane in the eighteenth century, then perhaps it devastated the trees that had been standing here. If so, these trees are roughly 200 years old. They stand more than 100 feet tall and many are 30 inches or more in

Yellow birch has the habit of seeding on fallen trees and stumps, and is then left with root "legs" when its host decays.

diameter at breast height (dbh). In forestry, tree diameters are measured at four and a half feet above the ground on the uphill side of the tree. That eliminates the flare of the butt end of the tree from the measurement. These giants certainly make an impressive forest to walk through and, with the meandering brook, a beautiful one as well. To learn more about old-growth white pine, see Canfield-Fisher Memorial Pines (page 9).

Leaving the pines behind, we crossed several bridges to Wright Reservoir and the Pond Loop Trail. This trail is *very easy*. There is a handicapped parking spot at the pond, and the trail is wide. Benches have been placed around the pond, and near one at its southern end is a large **paper birch.** I measured it in the spring of 1995 at 25.5 inches dbh. That's quite large for a paper birch, but it pales next to the **Vermont Champion Paper Birch,** with a diameter of nearly four feet (see page 315).

The trail passes over the earthen dam and circles the pond. The trees have been carefully thinned and trimmed on the dam's steep slope, a credit to the maintenance done by the town of Hartford Parks and Recreation Department. The Monument Trail leaves from the Pond Loop and climbs back uphill in 0.3 mile to the upper parking area. A sign at a footbridge over a spring-fed stream explains how Wright Reservoir collects water from winter runoff, springs, and streams in this small **watershed.**

As we neared the monument, an example of a well-built stone **waterbar** crosses the trail. Waterbars divert the water off the trail to prevent erosion. This helps maintain the trail and prevents excessive silt from finding its way into the reservoir.

Hurricane Forest Wildlife Refuge Park is a good example of what a town can do with public lands when there is a vision, a will, and a core of dedicated volunteers.

Paper (Canoe, White) Birch

Dendrologists (people who study trees) are at odds about the best popular term for this tree. To some, **American white birch** is just fine, but others protest calling it that, because **gray birch** is also white. **Canoe birch** is often used because Native Americans used its

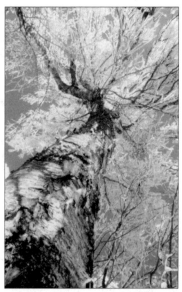

An old canoe birch tree, bearing rime ice in its branches. The average life span of canoe birch is about 75 years.

bark to cover their canoes. Its Latin name, *Betula papyrifera,* means **paper birch** (our preference).

So large were the old-growth birch trees that Native Americans are said to have been able to cover an entire canoe with a single piece of bark. In the old days, lumbermen would stuff its **thick waterproof inner bark** between their cedar shingles and log cabin walls. Its bark, however, keeps moisture in a dead tree, causing its wood to decay rapidly. As firewood, it is best to cut and split it quickly for drying.

Paper birch grows rapidly in cutover areas, often supplanting white pines after they are harvested. In a forest, it seldom reaches its full potential, since it is relatively short lived and shade intolerant. Once other trees overtop it, it rapidly declines. However, in a dooryard or open setting, such as that by the Wright Reservoir, its natural beauty often saves it from the chain saw or an early natural death. Grown in full sunlight, it becomes a handsome, majestic part of the landscape.

Champion Trees

The Vermont State Department of Forests keeps records of the largest known specimen of each tree in the state and publishes a list every two years. The largest tree of a species is commonly referred to as a State Champion. Under the auspices of *American Forests* magazine, a **National Register of Big Trees** is also published. It compiles the National Champion trees and Big Trees for all species in the United States. A tree's height, circumference at breast height, and mean diameter of its crown are measured and are used to give the tree a composite point rating. Thus, trees with lesser point totals than champions can be larger in girth or taller. These are registered as Big Trees and reported as well. Since many of these trees are open grown, they are most often located on private land, and specific tree locations are not published.

For those interested, the formula to determine a tree's point rating is:

Points = Circumference (inches) + Height (feet)
+ .25 x Mean Crown Diameter (feet)

Getting There

Hurricane Forest Wildlife Refuge Park is west of White River Junction. From White River Junction, go south on US 5. Turn right on King's Highway East immediately after passing under I-91. In about 0.25 mile, Wright Reservoir pond is on the left. Continue up the road another 0.25 mile and park on the left at the monument trailhead.

Affiliated Organizations

Managed by the town of Hartford Parks and Recreation Department.

Montshire Nature Trails
Montshire Museum of Science, Norwich

- 3 trails; 0.25–1.0 mile (10–45 minutes)
- very easy/easy
- admission fee to visit museum and walk the trails

The American Association of Museums called this "one of the finest museum sites in New England." Guide sheets to the trails are available on topics appropriate to the season.

The Wildflower/Fern Trail

In the spring, this is the Wildflower Trail, while in the summer it becomes the Fern Trail. As we exited the museum, we crossed the bridge to the left and turned right on the blue-blazed Ridge Trail. A few yards past the end of the parking lot, the Wildflower/Fern Trail turns right off the Ridge Trail. On our first visit in early spring, we saw two ferns that are green year-round. The **Christmas fern** has lustrous dark-green leaves, which makes it a friendly addition to holiday arrangements. It adapts to various soil and light conditions and may be found from swamps to rocky ledges. **Cinnamon fern** also remains green, although it lies on the ground from frost. It is named after its clublike fertile leaves that form in late spring. They are the color of cinnamon and distinguish it from all other ferns.

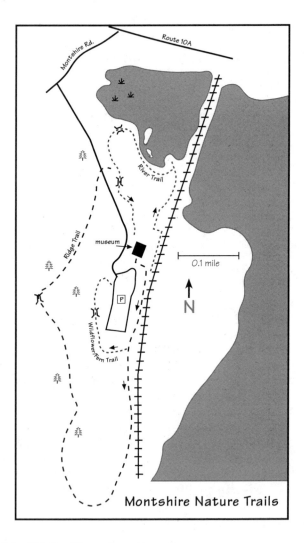

Montshire Nature Trails

Halfway along this short trail is a beautiful fern glen where a small stream cascades down a ledge. Among the many ferns to be spotted along this trail are **hayscented, sensitive, maidenhair, woodfern,** and **marginal woodfern.** On a visit later in the season, there was also a profusion of **ostrich ferns** (see page 322). The trail ends at the parking lot. Walk it in May and June to enjoy its large variety of wildflowers.

The River Trail

From the museums's main entrance, we turned left and crossed the small bridge again. A left turn brought us to the green-blazed path. We passed along the railroad track, over a small bridge, and came to a cove in the river. The museum provides several different *Trail Notes*

The award-winning Montshire Museum of Science.

for this walk. One that I really enjoyed is called "Cool Critters." It explores how insects survive winter, providing suggestions about where to look for them and describing the survival techniques used by different species. For example, **poplar galls** can sometimes be found on aspens. Galls are deformations formed in plants by insects who then use them for food and for protection while developing.

The *Trail Notes* describes one study in which **23 willow pinecone galls** were collected. These were originally formed by gnats, but only 15 of the 23 contained the original gnats. Inside the galls, scientists found six **wasp parasites,** 169 other guest **gnats,** and 384 eggs of the **meadow grasshopper.** That's 574 insects that had moved into 23 galls. A friend and fisherman showed me that when you break open common **golden rod** galls, you find a juicy larva—good bait for the end of your hook. In the winter, you can also look for cocoons, spiders, larvae, eggs, and even some species of adult butterflies in tree cavities, under the bark of dead trees (but please don't break the bark off), and under the snow in leaf litter.

Snow fleas—a type of **springtail**—are often seen on top of the snow. I spot them on sunny days in my outbound snow prints as I return from a walk. They seek out tiny suitable microclimates. They appear as tiny black dots, but can be recognized by their sheer numbers (10 million to an acre!). They feed on algae, pollen, and leaf mold.

The River Trail continues along the cove and then turns back toward the museum.

The Ridge Trail

From the museum entrance, cross the bridge and turn right. The blue-blazed Ridge Trail heads south, where it turns right up to the top of the ridge. After following the ridge, it descends to the entrance road.

At Station 10 in the spring or summer, the *Trail Notes* suggest looking past the big oak on the left toward a small, 10-foot hemlock. At its base grows **trout-lily,** recognizable by its brown-and-green splotched leaves. It is also called **adder's-tongue** after the shape of its leaves as they emerge from the ground. Many Vermonters call it **dog-tooth violet.** A new plant bears only one leaf annually for as long as seven years. Then, after developing a large root system, it finally bears two leaves and a small yellow bloom. Thus, in a carpet of trout-lilies, blooms only appear on two-leaved plants.

We crossed a second bridge and climbed a short hill. The woods change from predominately softwoods to hardwoods, and the large rocks among the softwoods disappear. That's because the soils here are soft clays. They were laid down as sediments in ancient Glacial Lake Hitchcock (see page 66).

The museum's *Trail Notes* provide excellent information on each trail and create an awareness of how nature operates cyclically. No matter which season you walk, the changing *Trail Notes* make this an ever-interesting place to revisit. Pick up *Trail Notes* at the museum desk where the admission fee is paid.

Ostrich Fern

The leaves of magnificent **ostrich ferns** resemble ostrich feathers. The vase-shaped leaves can reach six feet high, but when they first emerge, their **fiddleheads** (so-called after the way they curl on their stalks) are avidly collected. Their taste is similar to asparagus, but since they can be confused with other toxic fiddleheads, it is best to purchase them at a produce stand or market if you wish to try them. (Do not pick any ferns or flowers here, and please stay on the trail.)

Their fertile leaves stay erect in the winter and look like a brown-beaded feather, or lyre. Narrow pods containing the fern's spores rise upward from the fertile

Lush ostrich ferns catch the afternoon light along the Fern Trail.

stem, and, at two feet tall, provide an important source of food for **wild turkeys** when there is heavy snowfall.

Getting There

The Montshire Museum of Science is immediately east of I-91 at Exit 13. From the exit, go east on Route 10A toward Hanover, but watch for the immediate right turn on Montshire Road. At 0.2 mile, turn left into the museum. An admission fee is charged. Trails are open during museum hours, but the access road is locked after 5:00 P.M. No dogs or pets (other than guide dogs).

Affiliated Organizations

Montshire Museum of Science.

In the Area

The museum's purpose is to promote the understanding and enjoyment of the physical and natural sciences. It is self-guided, with a strong emphasis on interactive exhibits, from bubbles to the universe and from Tyrannosaurus rex to leaf-cutter ants.

Mystery Trail
Union Village Dam

- **0.75-mile loop**
- **1 hour**
- **easy/moderate**

This trail provides not only a great variety of nature and terrain, but a chance to understand some fascinating history by deducing clues from what you see.

The guide to this trail challenges the reader to be a detective, searching for clues to answer the questions it poses. We began by crossing a snowmobile bridge constructed in 1977 upon a much earlier hand-built stone foundation. We walked along the **Ompompanoosuc River** and followed a short spur trail to where it bends. There we saw the stone foundation of a **fabric mill** built in 1865. For 10 years, it produced more than a thousand yards of cloth a week. We explored it until we had figured out where the water wheel had been and how the water entered and exited the mill.

We followed the main trail along the riverbank to a meadow, where the stone foundation of the boarding-house for mill workers remains. Tall trees grow out of the foundation, though it is surrounded by meadow. Why? Because the meadow was a cow pasture. The cows—and sheep before them—grazed everything in

Mystery Trail

sight, but they couldn't get into the foundation. Near it are dead elms that succumbed to **Dutch elm disease,** a fungus spread by insects that was introduced from Europe in the 1940s.

We crossed the abandoned pasture, where **primary succession** plants are establishing themselves. This meadow provides a superb chance to see what much of Vermont looked like 75 to 100 years ago. Vermont's population peaked about 1860, when it began a 100-

year decline. Young adults left the farms to go west or look for better work in the cities. (The population didn't start increasing again until the 1960s, when many hippies moved to Vermont to form communes.)

A hundred years ago, about 75 percent of the state was cleared; today, about 80 percent of Vermont is forested—the most since the first Europeans settled here. Extensive land was cleared for pasture during the sheep boom (see page 328). We followed the path into a gully, where we turned right on an old road lined with granite fence posts. It soon brought us to the junction with an old town road. If you are short of time or energy, turn right here to complete the loop. We walked uphill to the left on the old carriage road. As stagecoaches, buggies, and horses used this road, a slab of

The foundation of the old fabric mill along the riverbend.

bedrock protruding from its middle was called many things: polite society, however, referred to it simply as **horse slip rock.**

At the turn of the century, the trees lining the road would probably have been the only ones standing. We examined the road and found its stone supports on the downhill side. Knowing how much work it still is to move boulders and pull stumps, even with heavy equipment, I imagined how difficult building this road must have been using only manual labor and draft animals.

We turned right at the top of the hill, but just before that is a large red oak with three boles. On the largest is a long seam caused by lightning. It now provides shelter for birds and small mammals and insects in the winter. The trail led us into a high field well into its first stage of succession. Its variety of grasses, shrubs, and seedlings is sometimes described as **edge effect.** The boundary between a forest and field grows up this way and provides a far richer habitat than either deep woods or cleared fields (see page 285). Here **foxes** pounce on **mice** and **grasshoppers; hawks** and **owls** seize **rabbits** and **rodents;** and **songbirds** catch unsuspecting **insects.**

At the field's end, we started downhill through an evergreen forest. We found the trail covered with needles, muddy, and extremely slippery. This area is a **deer wintering yard,** where whitetail deer take refuge. Tree boughs prevent the deep pileup of snow beneath them, and deer find it easier to move around. The trees also shelter them from chilling winds. Deer return to favorite wintering yards year after year, and conscientious woodlot owners leave such stands of trees when logging.

The torn edge of this juniper in the meadow indicates it was browsed by a deer.

We continued downhill and passed the beginning of this loop. Along the road is a marshy area. In addition to supporting a rich variety of plants, birds, mammals, and aquatic life, wetlands like these store water and help to prevent floods. They also filter pollutants, reduce harmful nitrogen compounds, and some help recharge aquifers and provide minimum flows for streams. From the wetland, the trail bears right to its starting point.

Vermont Merino Sheep: Boom and Bust

For centuries, Spain had a monopoly on merino wool that it enforced with a death penalty for anyone caught exporting merino sheep. Political upheavals in Europe, however, opened the door for enterprising American businessmen to obtain **merino sheep** flocks from Spain. William Jarvis, American consul in Lisbon, brought Spanish merinos to Vermont, where the potash industry had just collapsed (see page 23). Vermonters eagerly turned to sheep raising. The sheep thrived in the cold climate, growing thick coats of merino wool so soft that clothing made from it doesn't scratch the skin. The boom had begun. Everywhere, pastures were cleared and mills were built—just as you see on the Mystery Trail.

Landowners became fiercely proud of the quality of their sheep and wool, and Vermont merinos took international prizes. But unlike the Spanish grandees, owners accepted outrageously handsome prices to sell

A hand-hewn granite post along the old carriage road that the trail now follows

sheep to buyers in places such as California, Panama, Argentina, and Australia. As a result, worldwide supply far outstripped demand, and by 1867, prices plummeted and the bust arrived. Young men headed west to find gold in California or to find work in cities. In the space of five or six decades, 4,600 square miles—about half of all of Vermont—became abandoned pasture and soon began its succession back to forest, just as the Mystery Trail meadows have begun to do today.

Getting There

The Mystery Trail is at the Union Village Dam in Union Village. Go north on US 5 from I-91 Exit 13 and turn north onto Route 132. At 2.0 miles, bear right into Union Village. Just before the covered bridge, bear left to the Union Village Dam. Drive over the top of the dam into the Recreation Area. The trailhead for the Mystery Trail is located at the third picnic site. When the dam entrance road is closed, the trail can be reached from Thetford Center by walking in about a mile on the extension of Buzzel Bridge Road.

Affiliated Organizations

U.S. Army Corps of Engineers, Union Village Dam.

In the Area

Not far down the road from the trailhead is the Forest Management Demonstration Trail (next page). Walking it provides an excellent opportunity to learn about and observe woodlot and forest management techniques.

Forest Management Demonstration Trail
Union Village Dam

- **1.3 miles**
- **1.5 hours**
- **moderate, some up and down, hiking boots advised**

There is much to be learned by taking this pleasant walk through the woods to see the results of different forest management practices in different types of cover.

Discussions of how to manage forests are sometimes polarized between what are disparagingly called "tree huggers" and the forest products industry. Mark Rosenthal, a consulting forester, now regional project manager for the U.S. Army Corps of Engineers, decided that the emotions surrounding the issues needed to be replaced by knowledge. He created this trail to educate people on proven management techniques that preserve the health and sustainability of the land, while meeting resource requirements.

Follow the yellow blazes from the trailhead. For easier walking, we turned left at the first junction and followed the hiking trail, rather than following the stops sequentially. We gained some modest elevation and

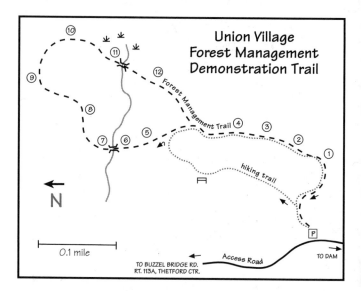

Union Village Forest Management Demonstration Trail

Forest Management Trail

hiking trail

N

0.1 mile

TO BUZZEL BRIDGE RD.
RT. 113A, THETFORD CTR.

Access Road

TO DAM

P

came to a bench, where we looked out on the confluence of the **Ompompanoosuc** and its **West Branch.**

Uphill, we joined the Demonstration Trail, blazed in red. We turned left to Stop 5 — an eastern white pine **cabbage tree,** whose commercial value was destroyed by the white pine weevil. A forester has three options with such a tree: (1) **leave** it standing to provide denning or nesting locations and food for many species of wildlife, as well as seeds for new trees; (2) **fell** the tree to open the site, although there is a possibility that this may cause significant damage to the surrounding forest; (3) **girdle** the tree by cutting through its outer, living layer (the **cambium**) all the way around it. This leaves

Forests may be managed for animal habitat. Newborn fawns, like the one pictured here, are left alone by their mothers so that her scent does not attract predators. The fawn instinctually freezes to remain camouflaged, while several times a day, the mother doe returns to move and feed her newborn.

the tree standing, but it disintegrates slowly and small sections fall to the ground, while also allowing regeneration.

On the way to Stop 6, the cover type changes to **hemlock, black ash,** and **elm,** reflecting the increasingly moist soil. At Stop 7, the white pines have grown tall as a result of terrain and the **aspect** of the slope (the direction it faces). Aspect is a key determinant of tree species, how rapidly they grow, and how healthy they are. Foresters produce a **site index** by comparing the average height with the average age of trees. An area with a high site index grows trees more rapidly, and can be managed more intensively and thinned more frequently.

Stop 8 is a **clear-cut.** There are a number of approaches to clear-cutting, and each uses a different tree selection principle and has a different result. Some approaches optimize short-term profit at the expense of forest health and sustainability, but others are used to optimize the productivity of the land. There is nothing right or wrong about clear-cutting itself; what is important are its objectives and the implementation of the principles that motivate it. Short-term profit can be maximized in several ways. One method is called **high-grading** or a **liquidation cut.** This occurs when all healthy, valuable trees are cut, leaving only unhealthy, poorly growing trees whose genetics will be perpetuated on the land. A second kind of destructive clear-cut removes almost everything to be sold, either as **sawlogs, pulp, firewood,** or **chips** for energy production.

Both types of clear-cuts remove many healthy trees that are not yet mature or at maximum value. For example, the current mill price for a 14-inch-diameter red oak is $750 per thousand board feet, but that rises to $1,175 if the tree is 16 inches in diameter. The dramatic increase in value is because wider boards can be cut from the larger tree. In good conditions, a 14-inch oak can grow to 16 inches in five years, when its lumber is more valuable and there is much more of it. Letting it grow those five years more than doubles the financial return. Thus, a liquidation cut is short-sighted not only from a forest health point of view, but from that of productivity and profit as well.

But clear-cuts are also valuable forest management tools. For example, they can change the **cover type** (or **species mix**). This might be done, for instance, to remove hemlock so that more red oak can regenerate, or to clear land in order to plant pine. It may also be the best solution to make way for new, healthy trees. A good example is the **salvage clear-cut** performed at Hapgood Pond after a stand of Norway spruce was damaged or blown over during a heavy snowstorm (page 155). The clear-cut performed here in 1981 was to allow an experimental planting of eastern white pine and hybrid aspen. Unfortunately, high mortality prevented the experiment's success. Foresters had wanted to determine if the aspen/white pine mix would attract grouse and to see whether the faster-growing aspen would inhibit the white pine weevil.

Stops 9 through 12 took us into **northern hardwoods**—sugar maple, beech, and yellow birch. This mix often develops when white pine trees standing on heavier soils are harvested or disturbed in some other fashion. At Stop 9 can be seen the damage done low on tree trunks when they are bumped by logs being dragged out by skidders. Sometimes it is necessary to leave a **bumper tree** to help maneuver logs around a corner, but it is best to avoid logging in the spring. That's when the bark is the most slippery and the most damage results.

Small **American beeches** at Stop 10 were left when larger beeches—victims of **beech bark disease** (see page 251)—were cut. No trees are growing at Stop 11 because of excessive ground water. This area is a small **kettle** depression with poor drainage. The use of **waterbars** (Stop 12) is important on logging roads and skidder trails. They greatly reduce erosion so that nearby streams and brooks don't silt up.

We rejoined the hiking trail and the beginning of the Demonstration Trail. At Stop 4, the stand has been thinned and pruned. **Thinning** trees at periodic intervals provides more room for growth for the residual trees, and they grow more vigorously. **Pruning** consists mainly of lopping off lower branches from the trunks of four-to-six-inch trees. This prevents knots and defects in the stem of the tree. Thinning and pruning are done periodically throughout the life of the stand. Growing by itself, an eastern white pine, for example, can take 80 to 100 years to develop high-quality timber; with managed thinning and pruning, that time can be reduced to 60 to 80 years.

When trees are grown, logged, trucked, and milled within the state, they make a significant contribution to the economy.

Approaching Stop 3, we enter an area of **quaking aspen**—the most widely distributed tree in North America. It is a fast-growing tree—three to six feet a year in height—but short lived. In the winter, its buds are eagerly sought by the **ruffed grouse.** At Stop 2, we enter a stand of **eastern white pine.** (Visit Hurricane Forest, page 309 or Canfield-Fisher, page 9 to see old-growth white pine.) It is a **catastrophe species,** establishing itself after wildfire or other site disturbance. The type of soil in which it grows determines whether it becomes permanently established or is succeeded by **shade-tolerant species,** such as beech, sugar maple, and hemlock.

Stop 1 is at Vermont's most valuable sawlog tree—the **red oak.** This particular tree grew in the open. That promotes low branching, spreading limbs, and an overall shorter height when compared with one that competes in a forest. The forest-grown tree must devote its energy to growing tall in order to capture sunlight in the canopy. It often grows with white pine in its understory, a result of past logging practices that removed mature white pines. When they were removed, the opening in the canopy stimulated white pine seedlings and released the red oaks to grow more rapidly.

We then headed downhill to the trailhead. This trail is an excellent example of using contact with nature to impart an understanding. Anyone in love with or curious about trees should include this walk on their list.

Crop Tree Release

Among the many approaches to managing a forest, one of the most popular today is **crop tree release.** Future crop trees—those that are healthy and have excellent potential commercial value—are first identified. Then trees whose canopies are crowding those of a crop tree are marked for cutting in such a way that about two-thirds of the crop tree's canopy is released. With more room and sunlight, its crown can expand and its growth will be stimulated (see page 191). This increases its value more rapidly. When the crop trees are harvested—in a **single tree selection cut**—the many trees remaining in and under the canopy will likewise be released.

Getting There

The Forest Management Trail is at the Union Village Dam in Union Village. From US 5, north of I-91 Exit 13, take Route 132 north. At 2.0 miles, bear right off Route 132 into Union Village. Continue to the intersection with the covered bridge. Just before the bridge, bear left to the Union Village Dam. Drive over the top of the dam and turn left behind the gate house. In about 1.5 miles, the trailhead is on the right marked by a large sign. Limited parking is available.

Affiliated Organizations

U.S. Army Corps of Engineers, Union Village Dam.

In the Area

The Mystery Trail, page 324, is nearby in the Union Village Dam Recreation Area.

Appendix A
Alphabetical Listing of Areas

Quick Reference Chart:

Region	Nature Walk	Page Number	Difficulty Level
Bennington Area	Healing Springs Nature Trail	1	easy
	Canfield-Fisher Memorial Pines	9	easy
	Branch Pond	16	easy/moderate
	Atwood Trail	27	easy
	Mt. Olga	33	difficult
Brattleboro Area	Black Gum Swamp	39	easy/moderate
	Sweet Pond	45	easy
	Fort Dummer State Park	52	easy
	Wantastiquet Mountain	59	difficult
	Black Mountain	68	moderate
	Putney Mountain	75	easy
	Bald Mountain	81	moderate/difficult
	Ledges Overlook Trail	87	difficult
	Hamilton Falls	94	easy/moderate

Hikes and Highlights

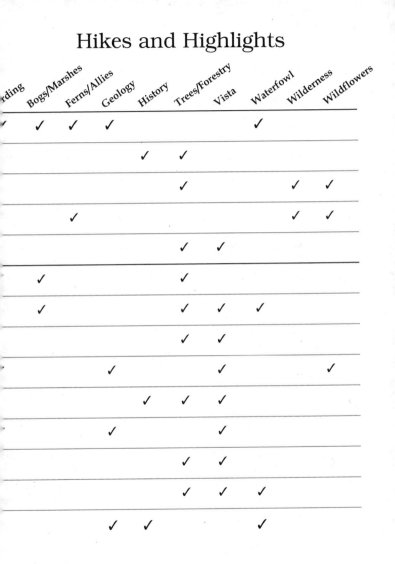

...rding	Bogs/Marshes	Ferns/Allies	Geology	History	Trees/Forestry	Vista	Waterfowl	Wilderness	Wildflowers
✓	✓	✓	✓				✓		
				✓	✓				
					✓			✓	✓
		✓						✓	✓
					✓	✓			
	✓				✓				
	✓				✓	✓	✓		
					✓	✓			
			✓			✓			✓
				✓	✓	✓			
			✓			✓			
					✓	✓			
					✓	✓	✓		
			✓	✓			✓		

Birding	Bogs/Marshes	Ferns/Allies	Geology	History	Trees/Forestry	Vista	Waterfowl	Wilderness	Wildflowers
			✓	✓					
			✓			✓			
✓	✓				✓	✓			✓
	✓								✓
					✓	✓			
	✓	✓	✓		✓				✓
					✓		✓		✓
✓	✓	✓			✓				
✓					✓				
	✓	✓	✓						
✓	✓	✓			✓	✓			
					✓				✓
✓					✓	✓			✓
			✓			✓			
✓					✓				✓
✓					✓		✓		✓

Region	Nature Walk	Page Number	Difficulty Level
Springfield Area	North Springfield Bog	223	very easy
	Springweather Nature Area	232	easy
	Pine Hill Trail	241	easy
	Lower Village Nature Trail	247	easy
	Wilgus Tree Identification Trail	253	very easy
White River Junction Area	North Hartland Lake Nature Trail	260	moderate
	Quechee Gorge	269	very easy/easy
	Eshqua Bog	275	very easy/mod.
	Communities Nature Trail	281	easy/moderate
	Gordon Welchman Nature Trail	289	moderate/difficult
	Amity Pond	302	very easy
	Hurricane Forest Wildlife Refuge	309	very easy/mod.
	Montshire Nature Trails	317	very easy/easy
	Mystery Trail	324	easy/moderate
	Forest Management Demonstration Trail	331	moderate

Birding	Bogs/Marshes	Ferns/Allies	Geology	History	Trees/Forestry	Vista	Waterfowl	Wilderness	Wildflowers
✓	✓	✓	✓						✓
✓		✓				✓	✓		✓
✓		✓		✓			✓		
✓	✓			✓	✓				
✓					✓				
✓		✓				✓	✓		✓
✓			✓			✓			
✓	✓								✓
✓						✓	✓		✓
✓	✓					✓	✓		✓
✓						✓			
		✓		✓					
✓		✓							✓
✓	✓		✓				✓		✓
				✓					

Appendix C
Organizations

Appalachian Trail Conference
PO Box 807
Harpers Ferry, WV 25425-0807
304-535-6331

Ascutney Mountain Audubon
  Society
PO Box 191
Springfield, VT 05156
802-263-5488

Ascutney Trails Association
PO Box 147
Windsor, VT 05089
802-674-5510

Bomoseen Nature Center
c/o Park Ranger Contact Station
Bomoseen State Park
Fair Haven, VT 05743
802-265-4242

Equinox Preservation Trust
Historic Route 7A
Manchester Village, VT 05254
802-362-4700 Ext. 895

Greater Falls Regional Chamber
  of Commerce
55 Village Square
Bellows Falls, VT 05101
802-463-4280

Green Mountain Club
RR 1, Box 650 Route 100
Waterbury Center, VT 05677
802-244-7037

Green Mountain National Forest
Manchester Ranger District
RR 1 Box 1940
Manchester Center, VT 05255
802-362-2307

Killington Resort
Killington, VT 05751
802-372-2007

Merck Forest & Farmland
  Center
PO Box 86
Rupert, VT 05768
802-394-7836

Merrell Hiking Center
Killington, VT 05751
802-372-2007

Montshire Museum of Science
PO Box 770
Montshire Road
Norwich, VT 05055
802-649-2200

National Register of Big Trees
PO Box 2000
Washington, DC 20013

New England Power Company
Bridge Street
Bellows Falls, VT 05101
802-463-3226

New England Wild Flower
   Society
Garden in the Woods
180 Hemenway Road
Framingham, MA 01701
617-237-4924

Southern Vermont Art Center
West Road
PO Box 617
Manchester, VT 05254
802-362-1405

The Nature Conservancy
Vermont Field Office
27 State Street
Montpelier, VT 05602
802-229-4425

Town of Hartford
Parks & Recreation Department
15 Bridge Street
White River Junction, VT 05001
802-295-9353

Town of Springfield
Department of Public Works
Town Hall

96 Main Street
Springfield, VT 05156
802-886-2208

Town of Vernon
Governor Hunt Road
Vernon, VT 05354
802-254-9251

U.S. Army Corps of Engineers
North Hartland Lake
PO Box 55
North Hartland, VT 05052-0055
802-295-2855

U.S. Army Corps of Engineers
North Springfield Lake
98 Reservoir Road
Springfield, VT 05156
802-886-2775

U.S. Army Corps of Engineers
Townshend Lake
PO Box 176
Townshend, VT 05353
802-365-7703

U.S. Army Corps of Engineers
Union Village Dam
RFD Box 98
East Thetford, VT 05043-9704
802-640-1606

Vermont Agency of Natural
   Resources
Department of Forests, Parks &

Recreation
RR 1, Box 33
North Springfield, VT 05150
802-886-2215

Vermont Agency of Natural
  Resources
Department of Forests, Parks &
  Recreation
Office of Information
RR 2, Box 2161
Pittsford, VT 05763-9713
802-483-2314

Vermont Agency of Natural
  Resources
Office of Information
103 South Main St., 9 South
Waterbury, VT 05671-0604
802-241-3655

Vermont Country Store
Route 103
Rockingham, VT 05101
802-463-2224

Vermont Fish & Wildlife
  Department
Nongame and Natural Heritage
103 South Main Street
Waterbury, VT 05671
802-241-3700

Vermont Historic Preservation
  Division
135 State Street
Montpelier, VT 05602
802-828-3226

Vermont Institute of Natural
  Science
RR 2, Box 532
Woodstock, VT 05091
802-457-2779

Vermont Youth Conservation
  Corps
103 South Main Street
Waterbury, VT 05671-0606
802-241-3699

Index

About the Author

Mark Mikolas lives in Putney, Vermont. His writing on nature, filmmaking, and photography has appeared in dozens of periodicals and books. He traversed the continent of South America by river on a year-long expedition, which he filmed for Venezuelan television. Wearing his other hat, he provides consulting, writing, and editorial services to companies engaged in continuous quality improvement and reengineering. However, his first love has always been the outdoors. When not at his computer, he is most often walking about in the woods. He leads a weekly group on "ambles" throughout southern Vermont and writes a column on hiking for the *Brattleboro Reformer*. He is active in many hiking, conservation, and environmental organizations, and serves on the Boards of the Southeastern Vermont Audubon Society and the Bonnyvale Environmental Education Center.

About the AMC

The Appalachian Mountain Club pursues an active conservation agenda while encouraging responsible recreation. Founded in 1876, the club has been at the forefront of the environmental protection movement. Our philosophy is that successful, long-term conservation depends on firsthand experience of the natural environment. AMC's 64,000 members pursue interests in hiking, canoeing, skiing, walking, rock climbing, bicycling, camping, kayaking, and backpacking, and—at the same time—help safeguard the environment.

The most recent efforts in the AMC conservation program include river protection, Northern Forest Lands policy, Sterling Forest (NY) preservation, and support for the Clean Air Act. The AMC depends upon its active members and grassroots supporters to promote this conservation agenda.

The AMC's education department offers members and the general public a wide range of workshops, from introductory camping to intensive Mountain Leadership School taught on the trails of the White Mountains. In addition, volunteers in each chapter lead hundreds of outdoor activities and excursions and offer introductory instruction in backcountry sports.

The AMC's research department focuses on the forces affecting the ecosystem, including ozone levels, acid rain and fog, climate change, rare flora and habitat protection, and air quality and visibility.

Another facet of the AMC is the trails program, which maintains more than 1,400 miles of trail (including 350 miles of the Appalachian Trail) and more than 50 shelters in the Northeast. Through a coordinated effort of volunteers, seasonal crews, and program staff, the AMC contributes more than 10,000 hours of public service work each summer in the area from Washington, D.C., to Maine.

In addition to supporting our work by becoming an AMC member, hikers can donate time as volunteers. For more information on these public service volunteer opportunities, contact the AMC Trails Program, Pinkham Notch Visitor Center, PO Box 298, Gorham NH 03581; 603-466-2721.

The club operates eight alpine huts in the White Mountains that provide shelter, bunks and blankets, and hearty meals for hikers. Pinkham Notch Visitor Center, at the foot of Mt. Washington, is base camp to the adventurous and the ideal location for individuals and families new to outdoor recreation. Comfortable bunk rooms, mountain hospitality, and home-cooked, family-style meals make Pinkham Notch Visitor Center a fun and affordable choice for lodging. For reservations, call 603-466-2727.

The AMC's offices in Boston and at Pinkham Notch Visitor Center stock the entire line of AMC publications, as well as other trail and river guides, maps, reference materials, and the latest articles on conservation issues. Guidebooks and other AMC gifts are available by mail order 800-262-4455 or by writing AMC, PO Box 298, Gorham NH 03581. Also available from the bookstore or by subscription is *Appalachia*, the country's oldest mountaineering and conservation journal.